Introduction to CGI/Perl

Common Gateway Interface

Practical Extraction & Report Language

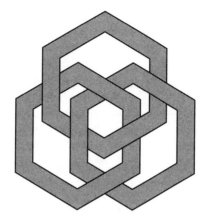

Introduction to CGI/Perl

Steven E. Brenner
Edwin Aoki

New York

M&T Books
A Division of MIS:Press, Inc.
A Subsidiary of Henry Holt and Company, Inc.
115 West 18th Street
New York, New York 10011

Library of Congress Cataloging-in-Publication Data
Brenner, Steven.
    Introduction to CGI/Perl : getting started with web scripts / by Steven Brenner and Edwin Aoki.
       p.   cm.
    ISBN 1-55851-478-3
    1. World Wide Web servers--Computer programs. 2. Perl (Computer program language) 3. CGI (Computer network protocol) I. Aoki, Edwin II. Title.
TK5105.888.B75   1996
005.7'2--dc20   95-50755
                                                               CIP

99 98 97 96   4 3 2

Associate Publisher: Paul Farrell
Managing Editor: Cary Sullivan
Technical Editor: Simon St. Laurent
Production Editor: Anthony Washington
Associate Production Editor: Ann Chen

"Fain would I dwell on form . . ."

—William Shakespeare, *Romeo and Juliet*, II.ii

"This may seem a bit weird, but that's okay, because it is weird."

—Larry Wall, author of Perl, in the Perl manual

Contents

Introduction xi

CHAPTER 1: Prelude to CGI 1

Saying Hello the Old-Fashioned Way .2

Behind the Scenes I: A Web Page .4

Scripting: When a Simple Hello Isn't Enough 8

Behind the Scenes II: Web Pages with CGI 9

Recognizing a Script When You See It 12

Review: Basics of Web Communication 16

CHAPTER 2: CGI Introductions with Perl .19

Perl Basics 20

Easier Introductions: Hello World with Functions 21

Perl Variables Part I: Scalars 25

How the Magic Works 26

Simple Subroutines 26

Perl Variables Part II: Arrays 28

Parameter Passing 29

Notable Quotes 32

Bonjour le monde 34

Perl Variables Part III: Associative Arrays 36

We Know Where You Live 39

Munging 40

Decisions, Decisions: Flow Control 50

Review: Perl and CGI 52

CHAPTER 3: Form and Function **53**

Formal Introductions 54

The <form> Element .55

Text and Password Fields 60

Radio Buttons and Checkboxes 61

Scripting 63

A <form> Letter 68

The <select> and <option> Elements 75

Multiple-line Text Areas 77

Submit and Reset 78

Comboform Processing 80

Origins of Inscrutability 81

But Wait, There's More! 87

Images 87

File Upload 88

Hidden Elements 89

Next Steps 90

Review: Scripting with Forms 92

CHAPTER 4: Controlling the Communication with HTTP and CGI **95**

The Hypertext Transport Protocol 96

The HTTP Request 96

The HTTP Response 98

Script Input 99

Extra Path 100

Extended URLs and Query Strings 101

Using Isindex Pages 102

The POST Method 104

The HEAD Method 105

GET vs. POST 105

CGI Environment Variables 106

Script Output 110

Output Headers 111

A Picture Is Worth a Thousand Words 114

Using Image Maps 118

Non-Parsed Headers 121

Review: Using HTTP and CGI .121

Appendix A: Solutions to Common Problems 125

Appendix B: Configuration Tips 131

Appendix C: The *cgi-lib.pl* Library 137

Appendix D: Online Resources 145

Index 147

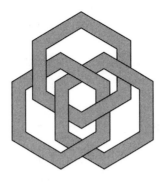

Introduction

It has been said that inside every big book is a little book trying to get out. This book is a testament to the truth of that adage. In *CGI Scripting with Perl*, due out early next year, we cover the use of Perl to create Web applications in great technical detail, featuring examples from a wide variety of gateway programs. However, we realize that many readers, especially those with less programming experience, are more interested in getting started with forms and other dynamic content as quickly as possible. For this reason, we created this book, which aims to describe the essentials of Web scripting in a compact, easily accessible format.

Introduction to CGI/Perl consists of four short chapters and four appendices. Each chapter builds on the one before it, and you should be able to read the book cover-to-cover in a few days. However, that doesn't mean you have to read the book sequentially. If you're more of the adventurous type, or if you have a specific problem you're trying to solve, you can jump around to find the information you need. The summaries at the end of each chapter can be used in conjunction with the brief descriptions of chapters given here to get a feel for where everything is in the book.

Chapter 1 begins by describing the relationship between a Web server and browser. We detail the interaction that goes on behind the scenes and show what happens when your browser requests a Web page from a remote server. We then introduce the Common Gateway Interface (CGI) and explain how the browser-server interaction changes with the addition of CGI scripts.

Chapter 2 tackles scripting in greater depth. We show how many of Perl's unique features make creating CGI applications easy. If you have a lot of experience with Perl, you might want to skim the first portion of this chapter, where we cover some basics of this flexible scripting language. On the other hand, those who are new to Perl programming might opt to skip the last section, where we delve into some of Perl's text handling capabilities. In any event, you will not want to miss the introduction of *cgi-lib.pl*, the *de facto* standard library for creating CGI programs with Perl.

Chapter 3 provides a look at how to build HTML forms. These pages, which differ very little from "ordinary" HTML pages, allow the user to enter data which can be processed by a CGI script. We start by introducing the HTML elements that collect user input and show how to put them together to create a form. We then examine how *cgi-lib.pl* streamlines the process of writing a script to process the form data. This chapter also includes a discussion of multi-part comboforms and how to create them.

Chapter 4 goes into more depth about HTTP and CGI, the protocols that govern Web communication. We highlight some of the ways in which script writers can use specific features of these protocols to enhance their CGI programs and further customize the user experience.

In addition to three standard appendices—which give useful troubleshooting tips (Appendix A), configuration advice (Appendix B), and a code listing for *cgi-lib.pl* (Appendix C), this book also features a set of Online Resources. Appendix D is a "pointer" to a Web site designed to accompany and complement the text. You'll find our code samples there as well as pointers to most of the public-domain and shareware software mentioned in the book, as well as more in-depth and up-to-date information on some of the topics we cover. You'll find the page at:

```
http://www.mispress.com/introcgi/
```

As you page through the book, you will surely notice certain typographical conventions we have adopted throughout the text. We use *italicized text* to set off new words or concepts, and ***bold italics*** to signify file names. `Bold monospace` text is used to indicate the names of Perl functions, while `plain monospace` sets apart HTML text, Universal Resource Locators (URLs) and Perl code. The Perl code examples given in the book are designed to work equally well under both Perl 4 and Perl 5.

This book is itself an example of how the Internet and World Wide Web can be used to more efficiently get things done. The text was written in California, New Jersey, and Cambridge, England, and drafts were distributed to readers around the world. All coordination was done via electronic mail, ftp, and the World Wide Web, with a lesser reliance on the telephone and express courier services. Final text and graphics were also sent to M&T Books in New York electronically; print was used only as a backup in case something went wrong.

But behind all of this technology, this book is really the result of the hard work of a number of people. We'd like to thank Paul Farrell for inviting us to write this book, as well as Ann Chen, Andy Neusner, Simon St. Laurent, Anthony Washington, and the others at M&T Books for taking our raw text and transmogrifying it into its final printed form. Their skill, as well as their encouragement and patience, are largely responsible for the volume you're currently holding.

We were also gratified to receive the support of many others as we embarked on this project. The short timeframe and constantly evolving subject matter could have taken a large toll (or perhaps, even larger toll) on its authors. The support of the Internet community, including many who use ***cgi-lib.pl***, helped alleviate this, as did the understanding of our respective supervisors Cyrus Chothia and Darren Yee. In particular, we'd like to acknowledge St. John's College, the MRC LMB, the University of Cambridge, and the Pocket Quicken Group at Intuit, Inc., for their understanding as we struggled to juggle our writing deadlines with our other responsibilities. We'd also like to extend our appreciation to those who took the time to look over the text and provided us with comments and criticism. Without the efforts of Bissan Al-Lazikani, Alex Bateman, Frank Chen, Willie and Kathy Chu, Purnananda Guptasarma, John Harvey, Michael Jennings, Anna Lindsay, Steve Nelson, Nancy Pearlman, and Jean-Paul Sursock, we would have been writing in a vacuum. Along with everything else, they enabled us to contact the Alpha Centaurions and speak Pig Latin without an accent. Of course, we alone are responsible for any errors or omissions in the text.

Most of all we'd like to thank those closest to us for their assistance and understanding. In addition to those already mentioned, who pretended to enjoy reading the book, we're especially indebted to: Bob Benedict, Mark A. Brown, Matthew Keating, Tony DeMatio, and THE GANG: especially, Selwin Blieden, Raphael Bousso, Tom Gallanis, Katharina Gaus, Mary-Hannah Jones, Thomas Niesler, and Terence Tsai. Thanks and love also are due to our families and grandparents for their role in this great adventure.

We'd especially like to acknowledge Edwin's wife, Diane Baek. Without her steady encouragement and unwavering support, not to mention putting up with Edwin's crankiness and 4 A.M. phone calls, we certainly would have lost our sanity long ago. Thanks, Diane, for everything.

Finally, we'd like to close with a few words on the first epigraph for this book, taken from that most famous of Shakespearean scenes: Juliet on her balcony. This line is more than just a dismal pun;[*] considering these words in context, we can find additional meanings that are relevant to this book. The *Riverside Shakespeare* interprets this quote as, "Gladly would I maintain formal behavior." Here, Juliet expresses her temptation to renounce her professing of love in deference to the mores of society. However, she rejects this course and impetuously seeks immediate but informal assurance from Romeo, thus propelling them both toward their

---

[*] In fact, it's several.

fateful end. In this volume, we too have chosen to dispense with formality in the interest of expediency and clarity, hopefully with less dire consequences.

If we dig a little deeper, we can divine another meaning to this quote— one which was almost certainly not intended by Shakespeare (though that fact alone has seldom proved a problem for most literary critics). Shakespeare's words come to us not by dint of their dramatic form, but rather in spite of it. That is, their capacity to elucidate and inspire are why they have endured to this day, as signified by our very use of this quote. This timelessness also illustrates an important point for Web page designers. Without valuable content, form assumes little import. In other words, no matter how elegant and beautiful your pages, without substance, they will be of fleeting interest at best. The pages with enduring value are those with both an attractive design *and* useful content.

We look forward to seeing your timeless creations on the Web!

Steven E. Brenner
Cambridge, England

Edwin Aoki
Sunnyvale, California

## CHAPTER 1

Prelude to CGI

The World Wide Web's phenomenal surge in popularity has been spurred by the explosive growth of available content. The ready availability of authoring tools combined with the Web's tremendous reach has made it easy for almost anyone to publish for a global audience. More significantly, the Common Gateway Interface (CGI) has enabled a new class of specialized Web applications that exploit the Internet's dynamic, interactive nature.

Dynamic Web pages are not built from ordinary HTML text files; instead, small programs or *scripts* create the HTML source text which a Web browser then displays. Because scripts generate documents on the fly, they are capable of incorporating information which changes or which cannot be determined in advance. They can also be used to solicit and interpret user-supplied data, retrieve requested information, or produce content which has been customized for a particular user.

The scripts that accomplish these tasks need not be difficult to write. Understanding CGI scripting, however, does require a good grasp of how the script receives and outputs information. This communications path is not entirely obvious because Web scripts don't interact directly with users.

Instead, they communicate with Web servers, which relay the information to a Web browser for display. These intermediate layers might seem to confuse the process, but it's really not that bad. Indeed, as we'll see, Web programming can be both fun and easy.

Saying Hello the Old-Fashioned Way

To understand how scripts interact with Web browsers and servers, we begin by reviewing a simpler interaction: how static HTML files are requested by and displayed to users. Figure 1.1 shows a simple HTML page which just says hi,[1] and in Listing 1.1 we present the source of *hello.html*, which produces this output.

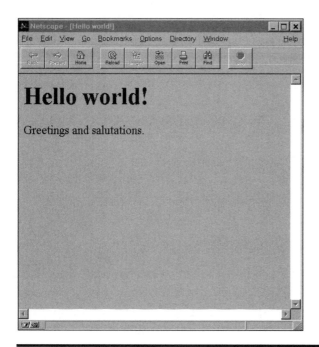

Figure 1.1 First impressions are always important. Our first page is *hello.html*.

---

[1] We are guilty of mixing metaphors here. "Hello world" may be the most popular first program, but a more common first Web page is "Under construction."

Listing 1.1 The contents of *hello.html*.

```
<html>
<head>
<title>Hello world!</title>
</head>
<body>
<h1>Hello world!</h1>
<p>Greetings and salutations.</p>
</body>
</html>
```

Once we've created the HTML text, it may seem that the process of delivering it to a Web browser should be a trivial task. But serving even a simple page like this one requires that a lot of coordination occur between the browser and the Web server on which the page is stored.[2]

The World Wide Web is based on a client-server model. This means, in a nutshell, that there is a *server* which provides resources, and a *client* which requests them. These resources might include computing power, a store of information, or a specific peripheral. The client and server (which are typically just software programs) may reside on the same machine or different ones. Furthermore, a machine which acts as a server to one client might itself be a client of another server. The important thing is that both client and server have agreed in advance on some mechanism that allows them to communicate with each other; such a mechanism is called a *protocol*.

To use a more concrete example, consider a local television station.[3] The television station has a number of resources, such as video tapes, live cameras, satellite feeds, and the like. When you turn on your TV and watch a program, the television set acts as a client of the broadcast

---

[2] We should perhaps be a bit more precise in using the term "Web server." While FTP, Gopher, and other servers can communicate with Web browsers, when we refer to a Web server, we mean a server which uses the Hypertext Transport Protocol (HTTP) to communicate with a browser. Examples include NCSA HTTPd, Apache, and the Netscape HTTP servers.

[3] We apologize to all of our readers who turned to computers (or this book) as an escape from television. We promise we'll be brief.

station, which assumes the role of server. Your client isn't tied to any specific server; you can change channels and get programming from many different stations. This is possible because all of the stations have agreed to speak the same "language," as it were, by broadcasting a specific type of signal on a particular frequency.[4] Any television set that understands this protocol can receive any station. So far, this setup may seem obvious. But what may not be as apparent is that your local TV station can also act as a client. In this scenario, the server is a television network which delivers movies, programming, or the evening news to the station. This example shows the way in which the labels "client" and "server" can change depending on the roles played.

As far as the World Wide Web is concerned, the role of the client is played by a Web browser, and the Web server is the software that delivers resources like computer files, images, movies, and sound to one or more browsers. There are thousands of servers throughout the World Wide Web, but they are all accessible from any browser because, like the television stations, they all have agreed to use a common protocol—in this case, the Hypertext Transfer Protocol (HTTP). HTTP is based on an exchange of requests and responses. Each request can be thought of as a command, or action, which is sent by the browser to the server to be carried out. The server performs the requested service and returns its answer in the form of a response.

Behind the Scenes I: A Web Page

We can now see the whole set of interactions needed to bring an HTML file from a server's disk to your computer's screen. Figure 1.2a shows the relationship between the user, client, and server, and Figure 1.2b details the communications between them. In particular, Figure 1.2b illustrates how the whole HTTP process takes place as a result of simple transactions consisting of requests and responses. When the user asks to see the "Hello world" page, the browser establishes a connection with the server and

---

[4] Well, all stations broadcasting in a particular area, of course. There are, in fact, several broadcast standards commonly used throughout the world.

sends its request using the HTTP protocol.[5] The request travels to the server machine, which then tries to locate the specified file. Upon finding the file, the server sends the client the file's contents, preceded by a set of headers which provide additional data about the transaction. Having finished with this request, the server then breaks the connection and waits for another request, either from the same client or a different one.

The response that the client receives is made up of a header and a message body. The HTTP headers contain meta-data not intended to be displayed to the user. Some standard header lines include a status code (indicating, for example, that the request was successful), the file's last modification date and time, and the file's `Content-type`.

The `Content-type` header line is particularly important because it tells the client how to interpret the information (picture, text, sound, etc.) encoded in the body of the message. It is the responsibility of the server to determine the file's type and return it in the `Content-type` header line along with the data. Typically, the server uses a mapping in which the file's extension indicates the type of its contents. In our example, the `.html` extension indicates that ***hello.html*** consists of HTML text. More precisely, the server knows (usually with the help of an extensions settings file) that the Media Type[6] of a file whose name ends in `.html` is `text/html`, so it sets the `Content-type` header line to:

```
Content-type: text/html
```

The client uses this header line to determine what do to with the contents of the response. For example, a browser may be able to decode and display a picture, but audio information would typically be played by an external helper application. In the case of ***hello.html***, the browser interprets each of the tags to display what we see in Figure 1.1.

---

[5] More details about HTTP transactions are given in Chapter 4.

[6] Media Types are standard Internet names for various types of documents. Some example types include `text/html` (HTML), `text/plain` (normal text), `image/gif` (GIF pictures), and `video/mpeg` (MPEG movies). Media types grew out of a standard called MIME; they are therefore sometimes called MIME Types.

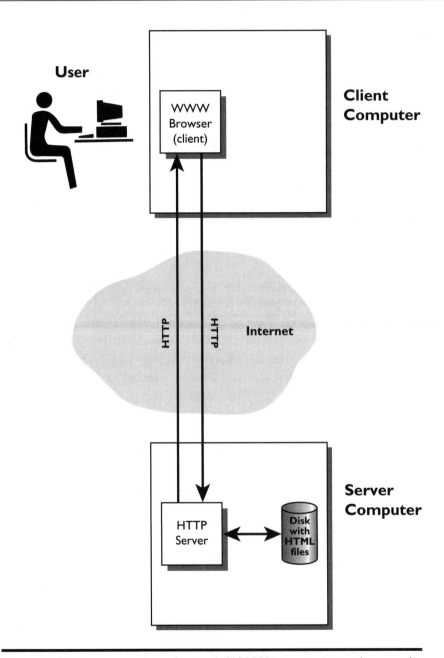

Figure 1.2a The components of a simple WWW interaction are the user, the client, and the server; the client acts as an intermediary between the user and server.

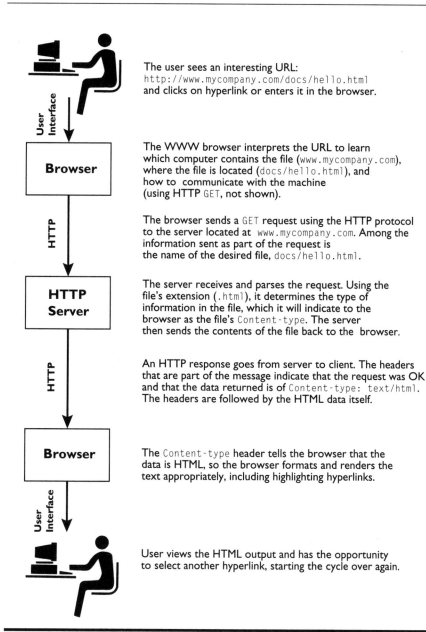

The user sees an interesting URL:
`http://www.mycompany.com/docs/hello.html`
and clicks on hyperlink or enters it in the browser.

The WWW browser interprets the URL to learn which computer contains the file (`www.mycompany.com`), where the file is located (`docs/hello.html`), and how to communicate with the machine (using HTTP `GET`, not shown).

The browser sends a `GET` request using the HTTP protocol to the server located at `www.mycompany.com`. Among the information sent as part of the request is the name of the desired file, `docs/hello.html`.

The server receives and parses the request. Using the file's extension (`.html`), it determines the type of information in the file, which it will indicate to the browser as the file's `Content-type`. The server then sends the contents of the file back to the browser.

An HTTP response goes from server to client. The headers that are part of the message indicate that the request was OK and that the data returned is of `Content-type: text/html`. The headers are followed by the HTML data itself.

The `Content-type` header tells the browser that the data is HTML, so the browser formats and renders the text appropriately, including highlighting hyperlinks.

User views the HTML output and has the opportunity to select another hyperlink, starting the cycle over again.

Figure 1.2b The basic information flow in a simple HTTP transaction is relatively straightforward; as explained in the text, the client simply requests a file and the server delivers it.

Scripting: When a Simple Hello Isn't Enough

The simple model just described works well for retrieving files but proves to be inadequate for more complex tasks. Most HTTP server programs can do little more than obtain pre-existing files and send them to clients. They have not been designed for complex data processing, such as retrieving information from a database or searching through text. Nonetheless, it is easy to see why these capabilities would be desirable and necessary, so the ability to extend the reach of HTTP servers is important.

One way to add features would be to make modifications to the server program itself. However, this process is unwieldy and requires access to the server program's source code and detailed knowledge of its internal operation. Therefore, most HTTP servers use a less direct approach to add additional capabilities. The server doesn't do the work itself; instead it delegates complex tasks to an external program or *script*.[7] In the case of database access, for instance, the script acts as a *gateway*, or intermediary, between the server and the data repository. When the server receives a request to access the database, it passes the request to a gateway program, which does whatever is necessary to get the data and return the results to the server. The server then repackages the information from the script, and forwards the information back to the client.[8] Typically, clients do not know (or care) whether the server handled the request internally or offloaded the work to other programs; they just interpret the returned result and display it to the user.

Clearly, in order to make this relationship work, the gateway programs and server must communicate with each other. The details of this interaction are specified by the Common Gateway Interface (CGI).[9] The CGI protocol defines the input that a script can expect to receive from the server, as well as the output it must return to the server in order to be

---

[7] Although they are subtly different, we use the terms "program" and "script" interchangeably.

[8] In a sense, the server acts as a sort of translator, taking data from either a file or a script and providing it to the browsers in a consistent and uniform manner.

[9] The "Common" in "Common Gateway Interface" derives from the fact that the CGI protocol is used by many different servers, allowing gateway programs written for one to work with the others.

understood.[10] What the script does in between the input and the output, though, is entirely up to the script. Therefore, CGI scripts can do much more than act as gateways for databases or other data repositories. Indeed, many CGI programs do quite a bit of sophisticated processing without accessing any external data.

Behind the Scenes II: Web Pages with CGI

With this background, we can take another look at "Hello world"—this time from a CGI perspective. Figures 1.3a and 1.3b illustrate how adding a simple script changes the flow of information.

As in our previous example (Figure 1.2), the user follows a hyperlink or enters a URL to retrieve the "Hello world" page. Though the destination given this time is a script instead of a file, the browser treats it no differently; from its point of view, the script is simply another address to be retrieved. To the server, however, the distinction is significant (see sidebar). Instead of retrieving a file, it executes the script specified by the address.[11] Upon starting the script, the server provides it with a variety of potentially useful information, such as the name of the machine from which the request originated and the type of browser used. The server may also include more specific information such as user input from an HTML form, as described in Chapter 3.

Armed with this information, the script must generate the appropriate data and return it to the server. The manner in which it accomplishes this task is of no concern to the server. For example, the CGI script may query a database, perform calculations, or twiddle its proverbial thumbs. Our example ***howdy.cgi***, shown in Listing 1.2, simply uses `print` statements to output some text.[12]

---

[10] Since this *is* a book about scripting, we take the script's point of view when we refer to input and output. A script's *input* consists of the information it receives from the server and the manner in which it is sent; its *output* refers to the information it sends back to the server.

[11] Our most precise readers will note that a script is also a file, and thus in the CGI script case the server must first locate and then execute the file, while in the non-script case, the server only retrieves the file. Although accurate, we choose to ignore this level of detail for the sake of simplicity. If all of this seems confusing, we invite you to ignore this entire footnote for the sake of simplicity.

[12] Readers who are unfamiliar with Perl can find more information in Chapter 2.

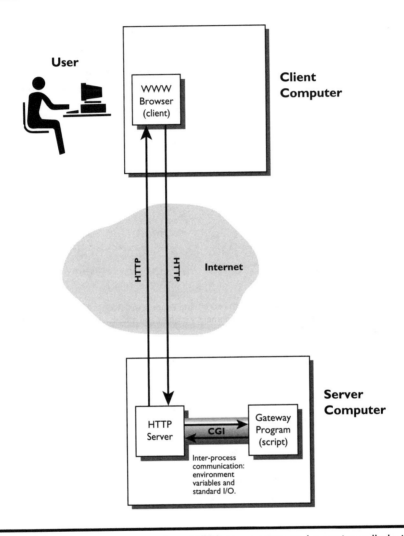

Figure 1.3a The components of an HTTP transaction and a script called via CGI. From the user's and client's points of view, the addition of a script on the server side is transparent. That is, the user and client interact only with the server; the server exclusively manages the communication with the script.

Figure 1.3b (on facing page) The information flow in an HTTP transaction and a script called via CGI. Because the server delegates some processing to a CGI script, two new steps are added to the handling of the HTTP request: input to and output from the script. Note, however, that the HTTP communication between server and client is the same as in Figure 1.2.

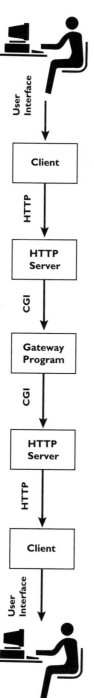

The user selects a URL that references a script:
`http://www.mycompany.com/cgi-bin/hello.cgi`.

The client interprets URL in the ordinary way.

`GET` message requesting `/cgi-bin/hello.cgi` is sent to `www.mycompany.com`.

Server receives request. Using the file's extension (`.cgi`) or its location on the server (`cgi-bin/`), it determines that it should run a CGI script.

The server starts the script and sends it information in the form of environment variables and standard input (`STDIN`).

Gateway program undertakes any necessary processing and then produces output. The program supplies a `Content-type` header to indicate the format of the data to the server, for example: `Content-type: text/html`. The headers are then followed by the HTML text generated by the script.

The headers (including `Content-type`) and data go directly from program to server.

Having successfully received data from the gateway program, the server relays the information to the client.

An HTTP response goes from server to browser. Included in the response are a status indicating the request was OK and the `Content-type` header from the script. Following the headers is the actual HTML text.

The `Content-type` header tells the browser that the data is HTML, so the browser formats and renders the text appropriately, including highlighting hyperlinks.

The user views the HTML output and has the opportunity to select another hyperlink, starting the cycle over again.

Listing 1.2 The simple CGI script *howdy.cgi* generates a header line and an HTML page. The first line of the script instructs the UNIX operating system to run the program with a Perl interpreter found at the directory location `/usr/local/bin/perl`. Readers who use Windows or Macintosh HTTP servers, or UNIX users with unusual configurations, may need to modify these programs slightly, as described in Appendix B.

```perl
#!/usr/local/bin/perl

print "Content-type: text/html\n\n";

print "<html>\n";
print "<head>\n";
print "<title>Hello world with Perl</title>\n";
print "</head>\n";
print "<body>\n";
print "<h1>Hello world with Perl</h1>\n";
print "<p>Howdy, world!</p>\n";
print "</body>\n";
print "</html>\n";
```

Recognizing a Script When You See It

How does a server tell that a CGI script is a script and not a document file? Often, without some help from the script writer, it can't. In fact, one of the most common errors encountered by CGI programmers is the failure to provide the hints necessary for the server to make this distinction. A confused server may generate a variety of different errors, depending upon how the server is configured and how the script was called. The most common result is that the text of the script (i.e., its source code, as in Listing 1.2) is output, rather than the result of its execution. You might also receive errors like "**can't POST to non-script**"—this message is particularly infuriating because posting to a script is exactly what you *are* trying to do.

These problems arise because there are no set standards for how a server should recognize a CGI script; consequently, different servers work in different ways. A model used by both the NCSA and CERN servers is to have a special directory in which all scripts (and only scripts) reside. The actual location of the directory on the disk and the name by which it is accessed over the Web (typically /cgi-bin) are specified in configuration files. *Any* request for a document in that directory or its subdirectories is treated as a request to execute that document as a script. Most servers support this model.

A newer approach is to use a filename extension to recognize CGI scripts, mirroring the technique used to determine a file's Media Type. The precise extension (and indeed the ability to have the extension specify a CGI script) is typically defined as part of the server's configuration. The most common extension for scripts is .cgi, though most Windows servers use the extensions .exe or .pl, and recent versions of Macintosh servers have used .acgi.

The use of extensions means that the CGI scripts can reside anywhere in the server's directory space, which has benefits and drawbacks. On the plus side, it means that scripts can be kept in intuitive locations, near related HTML files and other documents. On the minus side, spreading scripts all over the directory hierarchy makes it harder to keep track of all of them, in case they need to be updated. More importantly, if the server is configured to allow access to documents in users' personal directories (typically by mapping URLs with ~username to ~username/public_html), anyone can create and execute their own CGI scripts. While this may be appealing, it is common for inexperienced users to inadvertently write CGI programs with major security holes (especially if using shell scripts). Thus, a single user can potentially jeopardize the security of an entire server computer.

For these reasons, many servers come with extension-based CGI script recognition disabled by default. Even if enabled, many Internet service providers explicitly prohibit CGI scripts in users' space to avoid security hassles. If you try to run a CGI script in an area of the server where their use is not permitted, you may receive an **access denied** error. This message can be confusing as it also appears when a file's permissions are set incorrectly. Refer to Appendix A for additional troubleshooting hints.

Only a server can interact with a script. A client program cannot directly run (e.g., with the "open file" command) a CGI script; if asked to do so, the browser will likely display the script's source code. Because CGI communications take place between a server and a script, every CGI interaction must involve an HTTP server.

While the server doesn't care how the script generates its output, it does need to know the format of the output—the script's output is, after all, the server's input. Recall that when the Web server delivers a static file to the browser, it uses the filename extension to determine what to return in the `Content-type` header. This technique doesn't work for scripts, because a script's filename is unrelated to the type of information it returns. A script named ***getpic.cgi***, for example, may return an image as its data (`Content-type: image/gif`) while the similarly named ***getinfo.cgi*** might return HTML text (`Content-type: text/html`). It is even possible for a single script to output different sorts of data depending upon the context in which it is called. Therefore, it is absolutely essential that the script notify the server of the type of data it is generating, so that the server can pass this information on to the client. The first executed line of ***howdy.cgi*** does just that, specifying the Media Type that identifies the data in the message body. The `\n` combinations that follow the header information are translated by Perl into *newlines*. The first ends the line with the `Content-type`, while the second inserts a (mandatory) blank line that separates the header from the rest of the message.[13]

The remainder of the script simply outputs HTML text that looks suspiciously similar to the contents of the static ***hello.html*** shown earlier in this chapter (Listing 1.1), beginning with the familiar `<html>` tag and ending with `</html>`. All of this text output by the `print` statements is sent to the server which executed the script. The server captures the output, constructs a set of HTTP message headers (including the `Content-type` returned from the script), and sends these headers and the rest of the script's output to the browser. Upon receiving and interpreting the data, the browser is left with the HTML text shown in Listing 1.3, which it will render as shown in Figure 1.4.

---

[13] Actually, as we describe in Chapter 4, newline isn't quite correct, but it works.

Listing 1.3 The output generated by *howdy.cgi* not coincidentally bears a strong resemblance to the HTML shown in Listing 1.1.

```
<html>
<head>
<title>Hello world with Perl</title>
</head>
<body>
<h1>Hello world with Perl</h1>
<p>Howdy, world!</p>
</body>
</html>
```

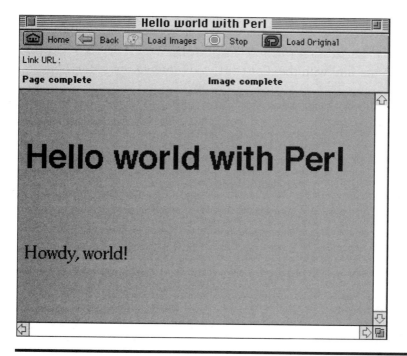

Figure 1.4 Despite the fact that this page was constructed by a script, it looks nearly identical to the earlier static page.

CGI scripts are quite flexible precisely because the server itself is not really involved in the process. The server's primary responsibilities are to start the script, send it the proper information, and pass the output back to the browser. It is up to the script to do most of the work. This division of labor leads to a protocol that is simple, yet powerful. We'll see some further examples of this power in the chapters that follow.

Review: Basics of Web Communication

We've seen that the display of an HTML document involves an interplay between the Web user, browser, and server. A CGI script complicates this picture only at the server end; the user and browser may have no knowledge that they are causing a program to run.

The programs themselves can perform a variety of functions and, as we've seen, can be quite easy to write. The most basic CGI scripts can produce an HTML page simply by generating a Content-type header and then printing the text of the document. Of course, like any program, a script can be arbitrarily complex, but even a simple program illustrates most of the basics behind CGI scripting:

- A Web client communicates with a server using the Hypertext Transport Protocol (HTTP). HTTP transactions perform simple actions like retrieving an HTML page or executing a script.

- CGI, or the Common Gateway Interface, specifies what information the server sends to a script and what the server expects to receive in return.

- From the browser's point of view, the execution of a script is identical to the retrieval of a static page.[14] All communication with the script is mediated by the server.

- Scripts are typically distinguished from ordinary HTML documents in one of two ways: either by being placed in a separate directory (/cgi-bin) or by having a file suffix of *.cgi*.

---

[14] Actually, there are cases when the client can have a pretty good idea that it is communicating with a script, such as when it is posting form data. We discuss this in Chapter 4.

- The output of each script typically starts with a `Content-type` header, which identifies the Media Type of the script output. Usually, this takes the form: `Content-type: text/html`. The header must be followed by a blank line.

The next chapter will take a closer look at how Perl and the *cgi-lib.pl* library make scripting easy. We'll put our ***howdy.cgi*** program on a diet and come up with a script that does the same thing in half the space. We'll even see how scripts enable us to create pages dynamically and communicate with users around the world.

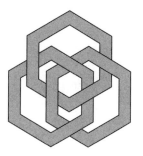

## CHAPTER 2

CGI Introductions with Perl

CGI scripts like the one shown in the previous chapter can be written in virtually any programming language. So why is Perl the language of choice for so many of the scripts in use throughout the Web? The answer lies in Perl's convenient syntax, powerful capabilities, and adeptness at handling text. Combined with its widespread availability, these features make Perl ideally suited to CGI scripting.

This chapter begins with a brief overview of the Perl language and demonstrates some of the ways that Perl can make the task of creating Web content less of a chore. We also introduce *cgi-lib.pl*, a handy library that can greatly simplify CGI scripting. Even if you've never written a Perl script before, the examples in this chapter could very well be enough to get you started. However, they are no substitute for a book solely about Perl. Because we focus more on Perl features useful for CGI than on CGI itself, those more experienced with the language may wish to breeze through this chapter.

Perl Basics

Perl is a funny language, rife with apparent contradictions. It will seem vaguely familiar to C programmers and shell scripters alike, but at the same time will appear relatively bizarre. Normally, people consider Perl to be an interpreted language because program execution basically starts at the top and continues line-by-line. But when a Perl program is run, it is actually first parsed and compiled, and only then is it executed.[1] This approach provides some of the efficiency of compilation while permitting the convenience and flexibility of interpreted languages.

Perl's power derives from a combination of the best properties of many different languages. For example, as with most interpreted scripting languages, commands in a Perl program need not be included within a function. Each line in a script is run from top to bottom; the first line of the script ordinarily will be the first to be executed. Contrast this with a C program, in which all commands must reside within functions, and program execution always begins with the `main` function. Like C, however, Perl is a free-form language. You can generally put as many statements as you like on a single line and put line breaks wherever you want. To tell where each statement ends and another begins, each statement must be terminated with a semicolon.[2]

This flexibility carries over to Perl functions and variables as well. Perl variables come in many different flavors, but all of them are case sensitive, don't need to be declared in advance of use, and are global by default. That is, unless you explicitly indicate otherwise, each variable will be shared across all the functions in a script. And speaking of functions, you don't need to declare them in advance either. Furthermore, many functions in Perl do not require you to enclose parameters in parentheses—a necessity for many programming languages.[3] Both functions and variables are covered in greater detail in the text and sidebars that follow.

---

[1] Nonetheless, it is possible to dynamically create a segment of Perl code inside a program and then direct Perl to execute that as well.

[2] Of course, rules were meant to be broken, so these guidelines aren't always true. For example, there are some special instances—such as formats—where the line breaks are significant.

[3] Sometimes, leaving off the parentheses can aid readability (as is typically the case with the print function), but it's usually better to include them.

Though easy to learn, the Perl language is very capable, as we'll soon see. Before diving in to look at any more Perl code, however, we should make a comment about comments. As in most scripting languages, Perl's comments are line-based, beginning with a hash sign[4] (#) and continuing to the end of the line. There is no way of making a true multi-line comment other than by putting a # on each line. Now that we haved bragged a bit about Perl's features, we can take a look at how we can use Perl to create Web content.

Easier Introductions: Hello World with Functions

You may recall that our first Perl CGI script, ***howdy.cgi***, (Listing 1.2) simply printed, line-by-line, a static document. Unfortunately, because the program ended up being more hassle (and keystrokes) than the HTML text it replaced, it probably failed to convince you of the virtues of Perl. Why would anyone write a program such as ***howdy.cgi***? Nobody would.[5] However, with the addition of functions, scripts can be useful even for generating HTML pages whose content does not change. Functions can eliminate much of the drudgery of producing syntactically-correct HTML text and automate much of the page-creation process, thus saving typing, improving consistency, and reducing the possibility of error. Listing 2.1 shows the text of ***hey.cgi***, which illustrates what we mean. Though ***hey.cgi*** bears little resemblance to our earlier script ***howdy.cgi***, it produces similar results, shown in Figure 2.1.

---

[4] Like so many of these special characters, the # symbol is called a number of different names. The most common of these include "hash," "pound," "tic-tac-toe," "sharp," and, of course, "number."

[5] Except, perhaps, the authors of a book about CGI and Perl.

Listing 2.1 The script *hey.cgi* uses functions to aid in the creation of a simple HTML page.

```perl
#!/usr/local/bin/perl

require "cgi-lib.pl";

MAIN:
{
  print &PrintHeader;
  print &HtmlTop("Hello world!");
  print "<p>Hey there, I'm functional!</p>\n";
  print &HtmlBot;
}
```

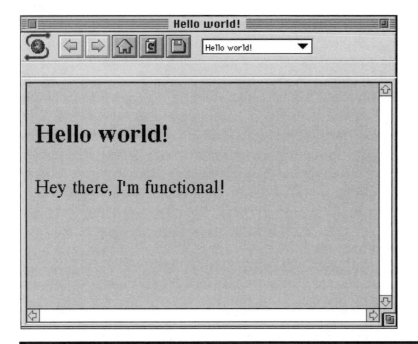

Figure 2.1 Output of *hey.cgi*. Despite the obvious differences in the source code, *hey.cgi* and *howdy.cgi* (Figure 1.4) produce similar results for users.

In order to see how ***hey.cgi*** comes about its results, we'll step through the source code (Listing 2.1) line by line. As with ***howdy.cgi***, the Perl interpreter runs through the script from top to bottom. However, the first executed line,

```
require "cgi-lib.pl";
```

does more than meets the eye. It essentially tells the Perl interpreter to treat the contents of the file ***cgi-lib.pl*** as if they were included in our script at this point. This treatment is analogous to the way the #include directive works for the C language preprocessor. By including libraries such as ***cgi-lib.pl***, we can concentrate on the specifics of what our script needs to do without getting bogged down in the mundane details; we delegate those to the library. The complete source code of ***cgi-lib.pl*** is listed in Appendix C, and we'll discuss it in greater detail soon. For now, it's enough to know that it is one of the most popular libraries to assist in the writing of CGI scripts, and as we'll see, it defines a number of convenient functions.

Returning to ***hey.cgi***, the next thing we notice is that instead of a simple list of commands, the program statements are placed within a *program block*. Blocks are regions of code enclosed in curly braces, optionally identified by a label. In this case, we've chosen the non-functional label MAIN to indicate that the code here is the core of the program. Unlike the main function in C, there is nothing special about the name MAIN; as far as the interpreter is concerned, it is just like any other block and not necessarily the starting point for the script. In fact, the block in this example has virtually no effect on the program's execution and exists primarily for convenience and readability. When we introduce subroutines, however, we'll see that blocks can be used to alter the flow of execution and provide enclosures for local variables.

Now we come to the actual program code itself. As we saw in Chapter 1, the first thing that a script must output is a header indicating the Content-type, followed by a blank line. Our ***howdy.cgi*** program just printed this out directly:

```
print "Content-type: text/html\n\n";
```

This doesn't seem to be onerous, but in practice, remembering the appropriate syntax of the `Content-type` header—and typing it properly—has proven famously problematic. Therefore ***hey.cgi*** generates the header using the slightly more mnemonic statement:

```
print &PrintHeader;
```

This line accomplishes the same thing as manually printing the `Content-type` header, but in a more convenient manner. The ampersand (&) symbol that precedes its name indicates that `PrintHeader` is a subroutine function; the actual code of the function is in ***cgi-lib.pl***. When called, `PrintHeader` returns the appropriate header line as well as the following blank line but does not actually print them, despite its name. That task is performed by the `print` statement, which sends the text to the standard output (called `STDOUT` in Perl). This output is then received by the Web server in the manner described in Chapter 1.

Once the header has been produced, the next requirement of an HTML-generating script is to output the text that begins the HTML page. Standard tags like `<html>`, `<head>`, and `<title>` hardly ever change from document to document, so they're perfect candidates for a function. In ***hey.cgi***, a single call to `HtmlTop` replaces all of the print statements to output these standard tags—the majority of the work done by ***howdy.cgi***. `HtmlTop` also takes a single parameter, in our case the string `"Hello world!"`, which is used as the page's title and first `<h1>` level header element.

The last couple of lines in our script simply print the "Hey there" paragraph and call the `HtmlBot` function to output the standard tags needed at the bottom of each HTML page. Though the `HtmlBot` function defined in ***cgi-lib.pl*** doesn't do much, we could replace it with another function that creates more sophisticated HTML page endings. It could, for example, display a menu or command bar of hyperlinks, give a contact address, or even show the current date and time. By putting our function in a library and calling it to terminate each page, we would be guaranteed that all of our pages would have a consistent look. Furthermore, if ever we wanted to change the design, we would need to make the change only once in the library, and all of our pages would be updated with the new information.

Perl Variables Part I: Scalars

Most programming languages have various data types, and Perl is no exception—but like almost everything else in Perl, there's a twist. Perl's simplest and most common data type, the scalar, replaces many of the common data types found in other languages. A scalar is simply a single item: integer, floating point number, string, or Boolean value; the precise type need not be specified in advance. A nifty feature of scalars is that they automatically convert between the different types as needed:

```
$number = 4;            # $number is 4, as you would expect
$string = "Hello";      # a nice, friendly string
$bond = "007";          # a more exciting string
print $bond - 2;        # prints "5" -- automagic string/number conversion
$scalar = "2" . "1";    # .(dot) is string concatenate; $scalar is "21"
$scalar -= 15;          # $scalar is now 6
```

These last couple examples may seem odd; hearkening back to the childhood riddle, "What do you get when you put 2 and 2 together?" to which the answer was "22." Perhaps the riddle was just preparation for our eventually becoming Perl programmers. But we digress.

In case you haven't noticed, all scalar variables begin with a dollar sign ($). Though this may seem annoying (and ugly) at first, it turns out to be phenomenally useful because it prevents variable names from being confused with Perl keywords. More interestingly, it also allows the variables to be directly substituted, or *interpolated* into strings:

```
print "The value of my scalar is $scalar.";
```

yields The value of my scalar is 6.

Even though words and numbers are represented using a single type of variable, there are some differences in how they can be used. For example, the symbols ==, !=, <, > (and others) are used to test numerical relationships (e.g., 1 + 1 == 2) while the corresponding operators eq, ne, lt, and gt play the analogous role for strings ("1 + 1" ne "2").

Listing 2.2 Compare the output of *hey.cgi*, shown here, to that of *howdy.cgi*, shown in Listing 1.3. Though they produce virtually identical HTML text, the use of functions makes *hey.cgi* a much neater and more compact script.

```
Content-type: text/html

<html>
<head>
<title>Hello world!</title>
</head>
<body>
<h1>Hello world!</h1>
<p>Hey there, I'm functional!</p>
</body>
</html>
```

How the Magic Works

Making use of unseen library functions in *cgi-lib.pl*, or any other library for that matter, may seem a bit mystical. Indeed, like magic (and like many aspects of Perl that we'll explore in this chapter), their use can range from simple sleight of hand to complex routines with many subtleties.

Simple Subroutines

Let's start our discussion of subroutines with `PrintHeader`, which is about as simple as a subroutine can be while still being useful.

Listing 2.3 The `PrintHeader` subroutine from *cgi-lib.pl*, though simple, is a useful way to make sure that the correct header is always generated.

```
sub PrintHeader
{
  return "Content-type: text/html\n\n";
}
```

A subroutine function is just a block, preceded by the keyword `sub` and a name. Functions can be placed almost anywhere in a Perl program, and the `sub` indicates that code should not be executed when the interpreter gets to it. Instead, it will be simply tucked away for use when needed.

Unlike some languages that have both functions (which perform some action and return a value to their caller), and procedures (which perform some action but do not return anything), Perl has only the former. By default, the value returned is simply the result of the last expression in the subroutine. Suppose the last executed line in a particular function were:

```
$four = 2 + 2;
```

In this case, the function would return 4, the value of `$four`.[6] If this is not the desired behavior, the `return` statement can be used to return a specified value. Often (as in `PrintHeader`), the `return` is not strictly necessary but is used simply to make the return value explicit.[7] Additionally, the return statement can be used to cause a function to exit before reaching its last line.

---

[6] The value of an assignment in Perl is simply the result of the assignment.

[7] If we wanted to create needlessly obfuscated code, we could leave out the `return` keyword. Since an expression like `"Content-type: text/html\n\n"` evaluates to the text string itself, if this were the last statement in `PrintHeader`, it would operate in the same way. The `return` keyword, though, makes this operation much clearer, so we think it is good form to use it. Perl can be obscure enough (see the last sections in this chapter) without introducing extraneous complexity.

Perl Variables Part II: Arrays

Perl can group a number of scalars together in an array; the entire array can then be referenced as a single variable. In Perl, arrays are denoted by the "at" character (@) and perhaps bear a stronger resemblance to lists in LISP than to arrays in C. Each array can contain any number of *elements*, which are simply scalars. For convenience, arrays can be assigned both to and from lists (denoted by parentheses):

```
@array = ("1", "two", 3);
($first, $second, $third) = @array;
```

Like scalars, arrays can be printed and interpolated into strings. Note that as in our first example above, an array need not contain scalars of the same type. This is an especially useful property when interpolating one array into another, an operation which simply inserts each of the elements of an array into another array:

```
@newarray = (0, @array, 4); # @newarray contains (0, "1", "two", 3, 4)
```

Individual elements of an array can be accessed by their indices, which as in C, normally starts at zero (although unlike C, the starting index can be altered). Also like C and many other programming languages, square brackets are used to specify the index:

```
$first = $array[0]; # $first is the first item in the array: "1"
```

A potentially confusing aspect of array *elements* is that since they are themselves scalar, the character that precedes the variable name and signifies its type is $, not @. This anomaly sets up the rather confusing situation in which one can have a scalar variable $array which has no relationship to the value of $array[0], a scalar that represents the first element of the array @array.

The highest index (the one which specifies the last element) of an array named @array is given by $#array, while the size of the array (generally one larger) is the scalar value of the array. These also work backwards; assigning a number to the highest index changes its size:

```
$last = $array[$#array];   # $#array is 2; $last is 3
$scalar = @array;          # $scalar is 3 (number of elements in @array)
$#array = 1;               # @array is now ("1", "two")
```

Perl provides enormous built-in support for arrays, making them very handy data types. We've only begun to scratch the surface of all of the ways in which Perl arrays can be used; for example, the language provides a number of special functions such as shift, unshift, push, pop, and splice to manipulate array contents conveniently and efficiently. More information about these can be found in the Perl reference manual (which comes with the language) or in books exclusively about Perl.

One of Perl's interesting features—and a further testament to its versatility—is that return values aren't limited to being scalars such as 13 or "Look ma, no hands!". Functions may also return an array, such as:

```
return ("fee", "fi", "fo", "fum");
```

Some functions take this a step further and can return either a scalar or an array, depending on the caller's need. The value of the (appropriately named) wantarray function can be used to determine which response to give.

Parameter Passing

Usually one wants to do more with a subroutine than simply produce some fixed output; a function which returned the value 4 all the time would be of limited use. Typically, functions also take some input values in the form of *parameters* and use them to generate the desired results. The ***cgi-lib.pl*** routine HtmlTop, shown in Listing 2.4, demonstrates this approach.

Listing 2.4 Functions Html Top and Html Bot from *cgi-lib.pl*.

```perl
sub HtmlTop
{
  local ($title) = @_;

  return <<END_OF_TEXT;
<html>
<head>
<title>$title</title>
</head>
<body>
<h1>$title</h1>
END_OF_TEXT
}

sub HtmlBot
{
    return "</body>\n</html>\n";
}
```

In Perl, the parameters that are passed into a function do not have any special names. They neither need to be declared in advance, nor must they be specified as part of the function definition. Instead, the special array @_ (the underscore character) holds all the parameters that are passed into a function. Each parameter can be accessed by its zero-based index; that is, the order in which it was passed to the function. Thus the first parameter would be $_[0], and the tenth would be $_[9].

Unfortunately, variable names like $_[14] don't roll off the tongue and can become pretty confusing. A good solution is to assign @_ to a list of named scalar variables. A function which takes three parameters could use a statement like:

```perl
($param1, $param2, $param3) = @_;
```

Or, better yet:

```
($name, $rank, $serial_number) = @_;
```

Note the great improvement in the mnemonics. Unfortunately, this solution introduces another problem. Consider the following:

Listing 2.5 Perl's feature of making all variables global by default can occasionally lead to unintended results.

```
sub NameClobber
{
  ($name, $rank, $serial_number) = @_;
}


MAIN:
{
  $name = "John";
  &NameClobber("Frank", "private", 12345); # $name is now Frank.
}
```

Part of Perl's flexibility is the ability to define a variable simply by using it, as in the first line in the MAIN block shown in Listing 2.5. But variables defined in this way are defined for the entire program; that is, they are *global* variables. Our assignment to the $name variable in the subroutine overwrites the original value of $name, "John", with the first parameter passed into the function: "Frank" in our example. One (impractical) way to avoid this problem would be to make sure that no two variables, anywhere in any of the subroutines in our program, shared the same name. A better solution would be to have a version of $name that was independent of any other variables elsewhere in the program.

The keyword local[8] does just that, and we use it in HtmlTop (Listing 2.4) to make $title a local variable. This effectively makes a new scalar

---

[8] Actually, in Perl 5, there's an even better solution, which is to use my rather than local. Technically speaking, local does dynamic scoping while my does lexical scoping.

variable $title, which is independent of any other similarly named variables and is used only until the current block exits. While the function HtmlTop executes, therefore, $title contains a copy of the parameter passed in. Any other $title that might be used elsewhere in our program is left alone. When we leave the function, the new $title is forgotten.

This mechanism is actually how the @_ parameter array works. Each function gets its own array that contains the parameters specific to that function; that is, the @_ array is implicitly local to each function. However @_ is a bit schizophrenic in that while the array itself is local, its elements are the original parameters of the function.[9] To illustrate, consider the case where one calls HtmlTop with a variable as its parameter:

```
&HtmlTop($myvar);
```

In this case, if code within the HtmlTop function modified the value of $_[0], the value of $myvar would also change. Since this may not be a desired side-effect, it provides another reason for why assigning @_ to a list of local scalar variables is a good idea.

Notable Quotes

Like PrintHeader, the HtmlTop subroutine returns a body of text as a single scalar value; however, it uses a different method of quoting—that is, delimiting—the string to be returned. PrintHeader (Listing 2.3) enclosed the returned string in double quotes ("); these are the most common quotes used in Perl. As we've already seen, strings within double quotes allow special characters to be represented by escape codes (e.g., newline is represented by \n). Another feature of double quotes is that they can *interpolate* variables; that is, wherever a variable like $billions

---

[9] In computer science terms, the elements of @_ are passed by reference.

shows up in a string, it will be replaced by the value of $billions when the string is evaluated:

```
$billions = "35 dollars";
print "We lost $billions\n"; # We lost 35 dollars, followed by a newline
```

On the other hand, the single quote (') doesn't do any interpolation on the enclosed text and only does very limited interpretation of backslash combinations.

```
print 'We lost $billions!'; # They'll be jumping out the windows
print 'This\nis\nugly\n';   # Displays a single, ugly line, complete
                            # with backslashes and n characters
```

The single quote is principally used to quote a single word or phrase, like its use in the first example to prevent $billions from being interpreted as a variable. It's easier to type than a double quote (no shifting necessary), and guarantees that "what you see is what you get."

A third variety of quote is the backquote (`` ` ``), which works like a double quote with an added feature. After the string is formed, its text is executed as though it were a command given to the shell.[10] The value of the backquote expression is the result of this command's execution. This usage can create potentially very dangerous security holes and therefore will be rarely found in CGI scripts. It is also not portable.

Quote marks only match up with similar quote marks, so a single quotation mark (or apostrophe) can be used as a literal quote mark inside a double quoted string, and vice versa. To use a double quote inside a double quoted string, you can either use the two character combination \" (shown), or employ a different quoting mechanism.

```
print "He said, \"She's lying\"\n";
```

---

[10] In UNIX, Perl commands for the shell are executed with sh.

An alternate quoting method which avoids the need to worry about quotes altogether is the *here document*. A here document begins with the characters << followed by an identifier (END_OF_TEXT in our function), which will later be used to terminate the text. Subsequent lines contain the here document's text, up until a line consisting of *only* the terminating identifier. By default, the text in a here document is basically equivalent to text enclosed in double quotes, but it has the advantages of readability, convenience, and allowing quote characters to appear within the text. They are especially appropriate for neatly delimiting large stretches of quoted text; we use one in the HtmlTop function for this reason. One aspect that may seem confusing at first is that the statement incorporating a here document appears on one line, including the semicolon at the end. The actual quoted text appears on lines *after* the semicolon.

To return to our example in Listing 2.4, the here document within HtmlTop contains a number of HTML tags and ends with END_OF_TEXT. Additionally, it includes two instances of the variable $title. Because the here document acts as a double quoted string, the $title is replaced by its value. In HtmlTop, $title is the local variable which contains the first parameter to the function. And in ***hey.cgi***, this parameter is the string "Hello world!". Thus, as shown in Listing 2.2, the string that HtmlTop returns contains two instances of the phrase, Hello world!.

Bonjour le monde

In our Web pages thus far, we've said hello three times and still haven't received any response from the user. It could be that we just talk too much, or maybe we're not speaking their language. In any event, it's time for a bit more interaction.

Whenever an HTTP server starts a CGI script, the server provides the script with a variety of information about its environment. This data includes the kind of server in use; where the client is connecting from; the revision number of the protocol being used; and other information which is more fully described in Chapter 4. We can use one of these pieces, the *fully qualified domain name* of the client machine to help us try to speak the user's language. The fully qualified domain name, or FQDN for short, is what is generally referred to as a machine name. It looks something like my-pc.mycompany.com, and we can use the portion after the last period (called the *top-level domain*), to give us a hint as to the country from which the user is connecting. Entries like edu, com, and mil are mostly in the United States, while uk and zw represent the United Kingdom and Zimbabwe, respectively. Internet machine names are not case sensitive.

The program ***world.cgi*** uses this information, along with a predefined table of greetings, to address the user in their native tongue. As Listing 2.6 shows, the first thing the program does after reading in ***cgi-lib.pl*** is to create a database of appropriate greetings. This is stored as an associative array (see sidebar), with the top-level domain name as the key and the appropriately translated salutation as the value.

Figure 2.2 The script ***world.cgi*** (Listing 2.6) uses CGI variables to give a user in Australia a response different from that received by a user in the U.S. or France. The actual HTML text that generates this page is shown in Listing 2.7.

Perl Variables Part III: Associative Arrays

Associative arrays are like normal arrays; however, rather than being indexed by numbers, they're indexed by strings. Thus, while a standard array will limit you to looking up entry 3, with an associative array you can use `"3.14159"`, `"pi"`, or even `"the whole kit and caboodle"` as indices. Programmers experienced in C may wonder what use such an array is; programmers experienced in Perl may wonder how C programmers can program at all without them. As we'll see in Chapter 3, associative arrays are used extensively in processing CGI information.

Like scalars and ordinary arrays, associative arrays are indicated by a special character, in this case a percent sign (%). And, as with arrays, each of the elements of an associative array is a scalar. However, in order to differentiate elements of associative arrays from those of normal ones, curly braces, rather than square brackets, are used to enclose the index:

```
$myassociativearray{'myindex'} = "myvalue";
```

Associative arrays are useful for establishing a relationship between two strings. In this usage, the string that is used as an index is called the "key," and the one used as the value, the "value." In an address book, for example, the names are the keys and the addresses are the values:

```
$addresses{'John Smith'} = "1234 Main Street";
$addresses{'Mary Doe'} = "115 Central Avenue";
```

A single entry in an associative array is often called a *key/value* or *name/value* pair. Like any other string, the array indices are case sensitive; they can also contain spaces and even nonprinting characters. Thus, associative arrays can be used to mimic multi-dimensional arrays:

```
$two_d{'2,3'} = "I'm element 2,3!";
```

Note, however, that since these array indices are really strings, they are sensitive to whitespace (e.g., '2, 3' is not the same as '2,3').

It is possible to assign associative arrays to ordinary arrays and vice-versa. The ordinary array represents the name/value pairs as sequential entries:

```
@ary = %myassociativearray;        # @ary is ("myindex", "myvalue");
```

When a list is assigned to an associative array, the reverse occurs.

```
@humps_list = ("dromedary", 1, "bactrian", 2, "camel", "1 or 2");
%humps = @humps_list;
$dromedary = $humps{"dromedary"}; # $dromedary is 1
```

Like other scalars, the individual elements of an array can be interpolated within double quoted strings:

```
print "A camel has $humps{'camel'} hump(s)\n";
```

Note the use of single quotes to enclose 'camel'. Double quotes are employed to delineate the whole argument to the print statement, so single quotes must be used to demarcate strings within it.

One final note: if an array like @humps_list contained thousands of entries, searching through it could take a long time. However, associative array lookups in Perl are very fast because they make use of hash tables. Accordingly (and also because it's much easier to say and type), associative arrays are often referred to as *hashes*.

Listing 2.6 The program *world.cgi* uses CGI information about the client to customize its message.

```perl
#!/usr/local/bin/perl

require "cgi-lib.pl";

# Associative array database of how to say hello around the world
%greeting =
  ('com', 'hello',           # US commercial sites
   'edu', 'hi',              # US educational sites
   'mil', 'greetings, Sir',  # US military sites
   'au', "g'day mate",       # Australia
   'fr', 'bonjour',          # France
   'il', 'shalom',           # Israel
   'mx', 'hola',             # Mexico
   'ru', 'priviet',          # Russia
   'is', 's&aelig;ll',       # Iceland
   'at', 'gr&uuml;ss gott',  # Austria
   'ke', 'jambo'             # Kenya
  );

MAIN:
{
  print &PrintHeader;
  print &HtmlTop("Hello world!");
  print "<p>", &WorldHello, "</p>\n";
  print &HtmlBot;
}

sub WorldHello
{
# This subroutine assumes that %greeting is defined in advance.
  local ($site,   # client's machine name - and then its location
         $hi      # greeting to send
        );
  $site = $ENV{'REMOTE_HOST'};
  $site =~ tr/A-Z/a-z/;
```

```
    $site =~ s/.*\.//;
    $hi = $greeting{$site};
    if ($hi) {
      substr($hi,0,1) =~ tr/a-z/A-Z/;
      return $hi;
    } else {
      return "<b>Error</b>: site $ENV{'REMOTE_HOST'} unknown";
    }
  }
```

This program has the now-familiar MAIN block, which, like the others we've seen, is quite straightforward. It begins by printing out the header with PrintHeader and the top of the HTML page with HtmlTop. The next line prints out a paragraph containing the results of *world.cgi*'s own function WorldHello which in turn returns a greeting in the appropriate language. Note that the print statement on this line takes a list of parameters; as shown in Listing 2.7, the members of the list are printed without the intervening spaces. Then the program finishes by printing the bottom-of-page items with HtmlBot.

Listing 2.7 The output from *world.cgi* when run by a user in Australia.

```
Content-type: text/html

<html>
<head>
<title>Hello world!</title>
</head>
<body>
<h1>Hello world!</h1>
<p>G'day mate</p>
</body>
</html>
```

We Know Where You Live

Now let's focus on the real meat of the program, the subroutine WorldHello. Recall that we want to look at the client machine's name and from this produce an appropriate salutation. To make this easier, we start by creating two local variables: the client's machine name and the greeting that we're going to return. Although our script is small enough that there are no similarly named variables in use elsewhere in the program, we declare the $site and $hi variables using the local keyword to ensure that no problems will arise should WorldHello become part of some other program in the future.

This function's first step is to obtain the machine name of the client machine by looking at the variable $ENV{'REMOTE_HOST'}. The %ENV associative array (of which $ENV{'REMOTE_HOST'} is an element) is something of a magic variable. It isn't a normal user-defined associative array but is created automatically by Perl when a program starts and is filled in with all of the shell environment variables which had been set at that time.[11] So, $ENV{'PATH'} is the current path used to search for files—what you'd call $PATH from the command prompt. The environment isn't read only; if you were to set $ENV{'PATH'}, you would end up setting the $PATH for any programs which you execute:

```
$ENV{'PATH'} = '/bin:/usr/bin';
```

But back to our script. As part of the CGI specification, the server has put the client machine's fully qualified domain name in the environment variable REMOTE_HOST. Thus, when we read $ENV{'REMOTE_HOST'} and copy it into $site, we're getting input from the server. Hurrah! We've finally got some sort of dynamic input from CGI scripting.

Munging

We're not quite done yet, as we still need to do some processing based on the client computer's host name and return the greeting.[12] We've got to isolate the last few characters of the machine name, change them to

---

[11] UNIX, DOS, and Windows-based machines have environment variables. Macs don't normally have them, so CGI scripts need to use a bit of glue to emulate them. Once the glue is in place, everything looks basically just as it would on a PC or UNIX. See Appendix B for more information.

[12] Munging (which rhymes with plunging) is the technical term for this sort of text manipulation. Well, in some circles it is.

lower case, make sure we can recognize the place (we don't have any appropriate way of saying hello to Alpha Centaurions) and then return the message with appropriate formatting. The good news is that this is easy in Perl and could be done in a single line.[13] The bad news is that the program looks garbled, as though it were line noise over a bad modem connection.

We'll walk through the code to produce the greeting one step at a time so that you can follow the program's execution. However, these features of Perl are rather abstruse, so unless you have some prior experience (or need to do exactly the same thing that we do in our example), this introduction probably will not suffice to write your own string processing code. Those who wish to learn more should consult a good book on Perl or the Perl manual.[14] Of course, many CGI scripts don't require this sort of processing at all, so for the time being you may wish to skim this section and then turn to Chapter 3, which deals with forms.

tr///

In ***world.cgi*** (Listing 2.6), the keys to %greeting are lowercase. Since we want to match the top-level domain name with the %greeting keys, we need to convert the name we receive from the server to all lowercase. In a typical programming language like C, this could be done by examining each character, determining if it is upper case, and then converting it to lower case if necessary. While this is hardly difficult, it is tedious and requires some knowledge (usually embodied in functions) about character-case and ASCII codes.

You could easily code this algorithm in Perl, but there's a simpler way. The translate, or tr///, command operates on a whole string at once, converting each individual character in turn. To make an uppercase to lowercase conversion, we use the following line:

```
$site =~ tr/A-Z/a-z/;
```

---

[13] Hardly surprising, since almost anything could be done on one line of Perl if it were long enough. In 3 lines of Perl, each of 80 characters in length, it is possible to write a program which is classified as a munition. See http://dcs.ex.ac.uk/~aba/rsa-perl.html.

[14] Links to the Perl manual can be found at the Online Appendix.

For the moment, ignore everything to the left of the tr. Let's call the text between the first two slashes the left hand side (lhs) and that between the last two slashes the right hand side (rhs). Each side represents a set of characters, and each character on the lhs is replaced with the corresponding character on the rhs. So, any occurrences of A are translated to a, and Z to z. The dash character (-) is not just another character to be translated; in this context it acts to expand the A-Z to fill in all the missing characters between A and Z and likewise for a-z. Thus, Q will be changed to q. This tr/// expression leaves characters not found in A-Z alone; hence, nothing happens to punctuation, numbers, or characters which are already lowercase.

The =~ symbol[15] in this expression isn't an assignment operator. Rather, it simply serves to indicate that tr/// operates on the variable $site. If $site and =~ were omitted, tr/// would act on the special variable $_ by default. Accordingly, the following code is a more laborious, but equivalent way of making $site lowercase:

```
$_ = $site;
tr/A-Z/a-z/;
$site = $_;
```

Often it is much easier to understand complex expressions which include =~, by imagining them without the =~ and the preceding variable, called the *query variable*. Note that unlike the shell and the sed command, tr/// and other text processing operators work on the entire contents of variables, not individual lines.

s///

The next line of the program looks even more bizarre:

```
$site =~ s/.*\.//;
```

---

[15] The second character of this is variously called tilde (because that's its name), squiggle (what it looks like), or twiddle (for no compelling reason).

Unless you know Perl or sed you'd be unlikely to guess that this statement deletes all the characters of $site up to and including the final period, thus reducing hippo.potam.us to simply us. Let's start by deciphering the familiar part: the =~ indicates that this unsightly operation once again acts upon the $site variable.

The actual function is the (appropriately named) substitution, or s/// operator. It is related to tr///, but rather than replacing each character on the lhs with the matching one on the rhs, it searches through the query variable trying to find a match to the whole left hand side. If a match is found, it then replaces that matched portion of the query with the complete contents of the rhs:

```
$weather = "A rainy day.";
$weather =~ s/rainy/sunny/; # $weather is now "A sunny day."
```

Substitutions only occur if the string on the left can be matched:

```
$weather = "A snowy day.";
$weather =~ s/rainy/sunny/; # $weather is still snowy
```

Changing the weather in a predictable way is nice, but you can do that just by flying from England to California. What you usually want to do is to match and substitute more general strings, without knowing in advance what they are. This is done by using *regular expressions* (regexps), created from a special pattern-matching language.[16] In Perl regular expressions, the period (.) is the most unrestricted character; it will match any single character:[17]

```
$weather = "Probability of precipitation is 80%";
$weather =~ s/..%/5%/;      # Only a 5% chance now
```

Note that the length of the strings on the lhs and rhs don't need to be the same, since the whole left is replaced with the whole right. In the

---

[16] Readers familiar with other UNIX utilities such as grep and awk will feel right at home with regular expressions. Note, however, that the Perl regular expressions are not always the same as the usual UNIX ones.

[17] Except a newline.

example above, ..% matches the percent sign and the two characters (80) which precede it. The 80% is thus replaced by 5%. However, consider what would have happened if the original probability had been 100%. The periods would have matched only the two zeros; the substitution would yield a 15% chance of rain. If, on the other hand, the probability had been 3%, the space before the 3 would have been incorrectly matched, causing a typographical error. To match numbers of arbitrary length, we need to use additional regular expression features.

Perl regular expressions have a number of metacharacters in addition to the period wildcard; for example, \d matches any single digit, \w matches "word" characters, and \s matches any whitespace character (a space, tab, newline, etc.). There are also antonyms like \D, \W, and \S which match anything but digits, words, and spaces, respectively.

```
$weather = "Winds at 9 mph.";
$weather =~ s/\d mph/50 mph/; # "Winds at 50 mph." now
```

By using these broader metacharacters, we can get close to our goal, but we're still not quite there. If our original winds had been 10 mph (or any other two digit number), then \d mph would have matched the last digit (0) and " mph", leaving us with 150 mph winds. If we had instead specified just \d instead of \d mph, only the first digit would be substituted, turning a 10 mph breeze into a fantastic 500 mph hurricane. What we need instead is to match the whole number, no matter how many digits it contains. To match a variable number of characters, we use the asterisk (*). It modifies the previous character or metacharacter to match zero or more occurrences of it—as many as possible. So, fu*n matches fun, fn, and fuuuuuuuuuuuuuuun. The expression .* matches any string of any length,[18] and \d* matches zero or more digits:

```
$weather = "Relative humidity is 90%";
$weather =~ s/\d\d*/10/;        # $weather is a comfortable 10% rh
```

A modifier similar to * is the question mark (?), which matches zero or one occurrences of a character. Using even more sophisticated (and

---

18 Well, most strings of any length. Remember that the period doesn't match newlines.

strange-looking) regular expressions you can specify a precise range of numbers of characters to match. Moreover, you can add additional parameters to the s/// operator. For example, putting a g after the last slash will cause all occurrences of the lhs to be replaced by the rhs rather than just the first one, and i makes the pattern-matching case-insensitive.

We have now collected enough tools to return to our original problem: deleting the beginning portion of the client's machine name. To accomplish this, we can use an s/// operator with no rhs, since deletion is the same as substituting the unwanted portion with nothing.

```
$weather = "It's pretty cloudy outside.";
$weather =~ s/cloudy\s//; # $weather is now pretty outside
```

In WorldHello, we want to match (i.e., eliminate) everything up to and including the last period in the machine name. Since an unadorned period symbol is already used as a wild-card in Perl, we must *escape* the period using the backslash to match a literal period; that is, we precede the period with a backslash (\.). Similarly, \\ matches a single backslash, \? matches a question mark, and * matches an asterisk. Hence, the expression .*\. will match anything up to and including the last period.

Putting this all back together again we have the line from WorldHello:

```
$site =~ s/.*\.//;
```

Line noise made functional.

Pattern Matching

The Perl slogan is "There's More Than One Way To Do It," and there are innumerable ways of extracting the last two or three characters of a FQDN to obtain the top-level domain. One class of solutions involves using the match, or m//, operator. Basically, the match operator is just the left side of the substitution operator: it tries to find a match of the regular expression within a string. The match operator evaluates to true if such a match can be made.[19]

---

[19] Actually, the s/// operator will also return true if a match is made (along with a substitution).

Like tr/// and s///, the match operator works by default on the variable $_. Unlike tr/// and s///, this command's name (the m) can be ommitted so it just looks like:

```
/huh?/                      # true if $_ includes hu, huh, or hubba hubba
```

One handy use for matches is in checking for user input. For example, the following expression will evaluate to true if the user said "y", "yes", or "yippie" (or "absolutely", for that matter), possibly with leading or trailing space:

```
$input =~ /y/;              # $input holds the user's response to question
```

Note that, as with s///, the regular expression need not match the whole string; rather, it just needs to match a substring.

Normally we'd actually want to check for both upper and lowercase yes responses, and for this we can use *character classes*. These are basically roll-your-own wildcards like the \d we saw earlier. Simply enclose the set of characters you want to match within square brackets, and the match will be true if any one of them match. It is also possible to match "everything but" a certain set of characters by simply preceding the characters in the class with a carat (^).

```
$input =~ /[Yy]/;           # match on Yes, y
$input =~ /[^Nn]/;          # matches any character except an n or N
```

The latter expression probably doesn't have the desired effect; if the user had typed no, then the match would evaluate true. (The o would match as not being N or n). We can fix this by requiring that the [^Nn] be the first character matched. To do this, we use the carat in a different context:

```
$input =~ /^[^Nn]/;
```

The first carat in this expression forces whatever follows it to be the first thing in the string. A dollar sign at the end of a regular expression can be used in an analogous way to force a match to the end of a string. The carat and dollar do not match anything themselves when they are the first and last characters in a regular expression, respectively. Note again that the two ^ symbols in this expression mean two different things.

Before we go too far astray, let's return to our problem of finding machines' locations from their domain names. We can reformulate this problem as matching all the characters from the end of the name up to, but not including any periods. An expression for this would be:

```
$site =~ /[^.]*$/;
```

The dollar sign forces the match to be at the very end of the string. The actual matching is done by the [^.]* expression, which finds zero or more characters so long as they aren't periods. (Note that the period is not escaped in a character class.)

This expression will match the required portion of the machine name; it will evaluate to true if the match is successful. However, we still need to retrieve the actual matched expression—the top level domain name. This is accomplished with one more smidgen of Perl regular expression magic. We just put the text we want to retrieve in parentheses:

```
$site =~ /([^.]*)$/;
```

If the match is successful, then the string matched by the expression will be stored in the variable $1. If we put more than one pair of parentheses in the regular expression then the text matched within subsequent pairs would be in $2, $3, etc.

To recap, we could have changed $site from having a fully qualified domain name to just its top-level domain by using:

```
$site =~ /([^.]*)$/;
$site = $1;
```

/([^\/]*)

Note: this is with match (m//) not search and replace (s///)

Incidentally, everything we've said about m// operator regular expressions also holds for the s/// operator. Hence, we could also write:

```
$site =~ s/.*\.([^.])/$1/;
```

The lhs of this statement matches an entire machine name and the expression in parenstheses will match the top-level domain portion of that name. The rhs of this expression, then, replaces $site with just the top-level domain.

Going back to the match operator, there is one more trick we can use to make the code "simpler." If the match operator is evaluated in an array context (e.g., the result of the match is assigned to an array), then it returns an array with what would have been ($1, $2, ...).[20] So, we could assign the country indicator to $country with the expression:

```
($country) = $site =~ /([^.]*)$/;
```

This may look horribly complex, but that's because it's doing a lot in relatively little space. Once you get used to programming in Perl, you will be writing code like this (and worse!) without thinking twice. Equally importantly, with experience, decrypting expressions like these will become second nature.

Substrings

All of the three previous string processing methods—the translate, substitute and match operators—work on whole strings. Frequently, though, it is necessary to operate on only a few characters of a string, for example, to capitalize the first letter of a word. Unlike C, strings in Perl are not character arrays, so there's no direct way to index into a string. Instead, Perl provides the substr function, which provides very flexible substring functionality at the cost of a bit of complexity.

---

[20] $1, $2, etc. are not set when you do an array assignment.

In short, `substr` extracts a portion of a string, beginning at the specified character position and continuing to the end of the string. Note that, as in C,[21] strings in Perl start with an index of 0.

```
$weather = "The weather is sunny";
$sun = substr($weather, 15);        # $sun is "sunny"
$sun = substr($weather, 0);         # equivalent to $sun = $weather
```

If we had wanted to extract only a few characters, we could also specify a length:

```
$sun = substr($weather, 15, 3);     # $sun is "sun"
```

Perl also allows us to assign to a `substr`, in which the substring is replaced by the value assigned:

```
$weather = "The weather is sunny";
substr($weather, 15) = "rainy";     # Need that umbrella after all
```

An interesting feature is that the specified substring need not be the same length as the string replacing it:

```
$weather = "The weather is sunny";
substr($weather, 0, 3) = "California";  # "California weather is sunny."
```

The `WorldHello` function uses the `substr` and `tr///` operators to make the first character of the returned greeting uppercase:

```
substr($hi,0,1) =~ tr/a-z/A-Z/;
```

The `tr///` is familiar, but this time it converts text to uppercase, translating anything from `a` to `z` to the corresponding `A` through `Z`. Because of the substring command, the `tr///` only operates on the first character of `$hi`, and so this line simply capitalizes the salutation to return.

---

[21] Perl is a flexible language. You can make strings and arrays start at something other than 0 by setting the special variable `$[`. If you set it to 1, then the first element in strings and arrays will be at index 1. This can potentially be convenient. However, because people normally assume that strings and arrays do start at 0, modifying `$[` is frowned upon.

We've now got well ahead of ourselves. WorldHello shouldn't (and doesn't) do the capitalization until it has succeeded in finding the appropriate greeting. Returning to the code (Listing 2.6), the lookup itself is simple once $site contains the lowercase top-level domain:

```
$hi = $greeting{$site};
```

If an appropriate greeting is found, WorldHello capitalizes it and returns the result. On the other hand, the script should produce an error message if it could not determine the client machine name, or if the name were in a country for which a greeting didn't exist in the database. To test these different cases and act appropriately, we need flow control.

Decisions, Decisions: Flow Control

Flow control is simply a fancy term for changing the order in which statements are executed. Rather than simply proceeding from top to bottom, execution of code in programs with flow control statements can jump around based on certain conditions. One example of this is the if statement, which is used in *world.cgi* to determine if a salutation was successfully found or whether an error message needs to be displayed.

Perl's if statement, like its C counterpart, evaluates an expression in parentheses and, if true, executes the program block that follows. (Unlike C, Perl requires a full block, in braces, after the if statement.) True means that the expression is neither zero, the null string, nor undefined. If the expression evaluates to false, the statements in the block are not executed:

```
if ($weather eq "rainy") {
    print "Don't forget a raincoat.\n";
}
```

The else statement, when used in conjunction with if, will execute its program block only if the expression is false:

```
if ($weather =~ /[Rr]ainy/ ) { # do a regexp match this time
  print "Don't forget a raincoat.\n";
} else {
  print "You can leave the raincoat at home.\n";
}
```

The **world.cgi** script uses if and else to do a little bit of error checking on the greeting it sends back. If, after doing our various munging tricks, the location can't be found in the table (maybe those Alpha Centaurions finally got onto the Internet after all), the program will return an error message. Our associative array %greeting has no entry for the hypothetical key αc. Consequently, the lookup for that site would have failed, and $hi would have been assigned the undefined value. This would also occur if $site were an empty string (which would happen if the server had for some reason failed to give us the client's machine name).

The if statement in WorldHello just looks to see if $hi is "true." In our case, $hi is either the right greeting (and thus evaluates to true), or it is undefined (false). In the first case, the if statement causes $hi's greeting to be capitalized and returned; in the undefined case, the else runs a separate piece of code to produce an error string. Note how we use variable interpolation to make the error message as clear as possible.

Perl has a full complement of flow control functions, allowing you to redirect programs' executions in most imaginable ways (and several that you wouldn't imagine). Some of the expressions, such as for, are particularly flexible. It is therefore somewhat ironic that many operations which would require loops and flow control in most languages can be done in Perl with one-line string manipulation commands. We told you Perl was a Quixotic language.[22]

But Quixotic or not, it certainly gets the job done. And all of those funny looking characters, munging operators, and powerful commands have allowed us to create our first page that varies depending on information we receive through CGI.

---

[22] This is itself rather Quixotic, for charging windmills is not generally considered to be particularly effective, while writing code in Perl definitely can be.

Review: Perl and CGI

We've rambled on at quite some length about Perl and CGI scripting, but we still haven't let the user get a word in edgewise. For that, we'll have to wait until Chapter 3. Even so, the two scripts presented here have illustrated a number of important concepts that are useful to people who create CGI scripts in Perl:

- The three types of Perl variables are scalars, arrays, and associative arrays. These are indicated by $, @, and %, respectively.

- Functions are blocks preceded by the `sub` keyword and a name. Functions are called by preceding their name with a &. Function parameters are put in the special array @_.

- The library **cgi-lib.pl** provides a number of useful functions, including `PrintHeader`, `HtmlTop`, and `HtmlBot`.

- Perl quoting comes in several flavors. The most popular is double quoting, which will interpolate variables. Here documents are an useful way to include a large amount of text in a script.

- As part of the CGI specification, the server provides the script with information in the form of environment variables, accessible through the `%ENV` associative array.

- Perl's string manipulation abilities, with their heavy dose of regular expressions, can be powerful tools that perform complicated text handling operations.

Bearing these points in mind, scripts can easily be created to show external information, such as the weather or time, or can be used to control devices like a camera or model train.[23]

---

[23] An impressive list of devices connected to the Internet can be found at
`http://www.yahoo.com/Computers_and_Internet/Internet/Interesting_Devices_Connected_to_the_Net/`.

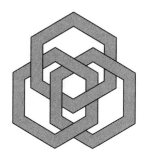

## CHAPTER 3

Form and Function

Up to this point, we've talked a lot about dynamic content but have not really done much about it. We began by showing how Perl and *cgi-lib.pl* can ease the task of generating HTML text and illustrated how CGI environment variables can be employed to create output better suited to the needs of our users. However, our earlier examples lacked one of the most significant aspects of the World Wide Web—true interactivity. Interactive pages solicit information from the user and, based on that information, perform an appropriate action. To make this happen, two things are necessary: an HTML form to actually gather the data, and a script to process it and return a result.

Forms are simply HTML pages that employ a variety of user-interface widgets[1] to gather input from the user. These widgets, including text input fields, radio buttons, and checkboxes, will be immediately familiar to most computer users. Similarly, because forms are made up of the same HTML building blocks as non-interactive pages, those who have previously created static HTML pages need learn only a few new tricks to master

---

[1] A widget is similar to a gizmo or gadget. In this context, it refers to a component that makes up part of a user-interface.

forms. A form uses special tags to determine its appearance and to indicate how the completed form data should be transmitted from the client to the server, and eventually to a script.

It is the script's job to interpret the form data and synthesize a response. To obtain the form information, the script communicates with the server using the CGI protocol. After performing any necessary processing, the script creates output that is sent back to the server for delivery to the browser. We've already seen how Perl and ***cgi-lib.pl*** can simplify the creation of dynamic output, but, as this chapter demonstrates, they are even more helpful in dealing with forms input. Before we tackle forms processing, though, let's take a look at how an HTML form is put together.

Formal Introductions

Our first form, shown in Figure 3.1, translates the phrase, "Hello, <name>. How are you?" into a number of different languages. A bank of radio buttons allows the user to choose the desired language, and the name is supplied by a text input field. Additionally, a checkbox is provided that allows the user to see all of the form data passed to the script. When the user has completed the form, he or she presses a button at the bottom to *submit* the results to the server for processing.

The HTML source which produces Figure 3.1 is given in Listing 3.1. It looks essentially like that of the other Web pages we've seen, with the exception of a few new elements that govern the form's appearance and behavior. Table 3.1, at the end of this chapter, summarizes these new elements. In particular, the `<form>` tag and its terminating tag `</form>` define a logical portion of the page as an interactive HTML form. Between these two tags, page designers can use normal HTML elements as well as special form elements like `<input>` to create the form's user interface. Unlike most tags, which can appear anywhere on a page, these form-specific tags are only valid within a form element bracketed by `<form>` and `</form>`.[2] The next few sections examine each of these elements in greater detail.

---

[2] We use the words "form" and "page" almost interchangeably. Actually, however, a single page can have multiple (unnested) forms bracketed by `<form>` and `</form>` tags, each with its own elements and processing script. In this case, each form is treated independently. They do not interact with each other in any way, and the user can only submit data to one at a time.

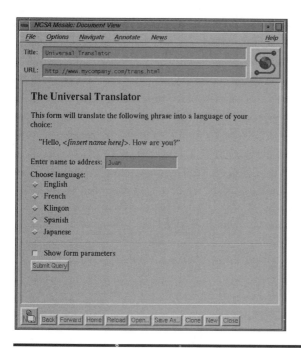

Figure 3.1 Our first interactive form uses simple interface elements to get input from the user.

The <form> Element

As well as simply marking the beginning and end of a form, the <form> element also establishes the relationship between the form page and the script that will be called to process the form data. The form's action attribute specifies the address of the script. Usually, as in our example, the address is simply the name of an executable file (***trans.cgi*** in this case) on the same machine as the server, but it could be a complete URL to any accessible script. The <form> element's remaining attributes, method and enctype, specify how the script will receive the completed form data.

The <form>'s method attribute determines which HTTP method—GET or POST—the browser should use to deliver information to the server. In brief, the GET method delivers form data by appending it to the URL of

At FSU GET confuses cgiwrap; use POST !

the script, whereas the POST method sends it as a body of text. Chapter 4 explains how GET and POST work and discusses the reasons why you might choose to use one rather than the other. But we don't need to worry too much about the distinction here, because ***cgi-lib.pl*** automatically handles all of the complexities of reading in the form data regardless of which method is used. For our current example, we've chosen to use the GET method.

The <form> tag's only other attribute, the enctype, is one that we don't use in our sample script. The enctype specifies the encoding that the browser should perform on the form data before sending it to the server. These encodings are necessary so that special characters, such as spaces and punctuation, can be delivered reliably to the script. As in our example, the enctype attribute is almost always omitted because its default value, application/x-www-form-urlencoded, is correct for most forms. The only time you must specify an enctype of multipart/form-data (the only other defined value) is in creating a form that contains the newly defined file <input> element, described at the end of this chapter.*

SYNTAX NOTE: <form> element

Encloses a block of text that represents a form and specifies the script to which the form will send the completed information.

Attributes:

method = [GET | POST], how to send the data to the script.

action = the URL of a CGI script to process the data. If not given, defaults to the same URL as the form.

enctype = [application/x-www-form-urlencoded | multipart/form-data*]. Defaults to application/x-www-form-urlencoded. The way in which the form data is encoded before delivery to the script.

---

* Features supported by Netscape version 2.0 that are not part of the HTML 2.0 standard, such as multipart/form-data, are denoted by asterisks.

Listing 3.1 The form *trans.html* makes use of a number of form-specific tags.

```
<html>
<head>
<title>Universal Translator</title>
</head>
<body>
<h1>The Universal Translator</h1>
<p> This form will translate the following phrase
into a language of your choice:</p>
<blockquote>"Hello, &lt;<i>[insert name here]</i>&gt;.  How are you?"
</blockquote>

<form method=get action="trans.cgi">
Enter name:
<input type=text name="who">
<br>
Choose language:
<br><input type=radio name="lang" value=english> English
<br><input type=radio name="lang" value=french > French
<br><input type=radio name="lang" value=klingon> Klingon
<br><input type=radio name="lang" value=spanish checked> Spanish
<br><input type=radio name="lang" value=japan  > Japanese
<br>
<input type=checkbox name="params" value=1> Show form parameters<br>
<input type=submit>
<br>
</form>
</body>
</html>
```
[handwritten annotation: "post" above "get" in the form method line]

The steps involved in filling out and processing a form are shown graphically in Figure 3.2. Though they may seem complicated, they really are just a combination of things we've seen earlier. In the first phase of our example, the client retrieves and displays the form. To do so, the client sends the server the address of an HTML document to fetch, **trans.html** in our example. The server locates the file and returns its contents to the browser, which interprets the HTML data to show the appropriate form interface.

The second phase begins after the user fills out the form and presses the submit button. At this point, the client bundles up the form data and sends it to the server, instructing the server to run the script specified in the form's `action` attribute. The server complies, executing the program and passing along the data provided by the browser. After processing the data, the script returns some output to the server, preceded by headers such as the `Content-type`. Finally, the server passes this output back to the client browser, which displays the script's results to the user.

While the `<form>` tag is necessary to set up the framework for the form, by itself it doesn't cause anything to be displayed to the user. To actually solicit user feedback, our form uses `<input>` elements. These elements can create a wide variety of interface widgets; their `type` attribute is used to specify each element's appearance and features.[3]

There are two attributes besides `type` which are general to all `<input>` elements: `name` and `value`. These are crucial because they comprise the only information that the script receives from the form. The `name` attribute

---

Figure 3.2 (on facing page) In order to display a form and then process its results, two independent HTTP transactions are necessary: the first retrieves the form to display, and the second actually processes the data. Readers may feel some *déja vu* here, as the first transaction is identical to that shown in Figure 1.2b, and the second differs from that shown in Figure 1.3b only in that form data is also submitted with the request.

---

[3] Of course, as with all HTML text, the *exact* rendering of an item on screen is dependent on the browser being used, but the `type` field determines the principal functionality for each element.

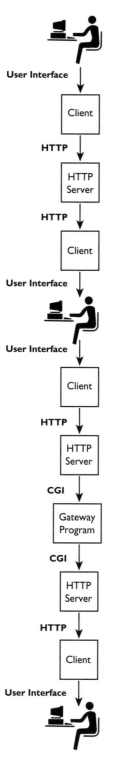

Wanting to know how to say hello in Spanish, the user selects the translation form's URL
`http://www.mycompany.com/trans.html`

User Interface

Client

HTTP

`GET` message requesting `/trans.html` is sent to `www.mycompany.com`.

HTTP Server

HTTP

Server receives request. Based on the `.html` extension, server retrieves the file and returns its contents to the server, preceded by the `Content-type` header and status code.

Client

User Interface

Client receives and displays the data. The `<form>` and `<input>` tags indicate that the browser should render a form with the appropriate user interface elements.

User Interface

User fills out the form and presses the submit button to send the data to the server.

Client

The client looks at the form's action attribute for the destination address. GET, given in the form's method, tells the client to append the form data to the resource address:
  `/trans.cgi?who=Juan&lang=spanish&params=1`

HTTP

HTTP Server

Server receives request. The file extension `.cgi` indicates it should run a CGI script.

CGI

The server starts the script and sends it information via environment variables.

Gateway Program

The script processes the form results and returns HTML text. The header preceding the text contains the line `Content-type: text/html` to indicate that the forms output is HTML text.

CGI

HTTP Server

The server relays the information to the client.

HTTP

The HTTP response includes a status code and additional headers, along with the text from the script.

Client

The `Content-type` header tells the browser that the data is HTML, so the browser formats and renders the text appropriately, including rendering hyperlinks.

User Interface

User views the HTML text to learn that hello in Spanish is "Hola."

identifies each user interface element, and the `value` contains associated information that is also sent to the script. Upon submission of the form, the browser assembles the form data into a series of `name`/`value` pairs for delivery to the server and thence to the script. The script can retrieve the `value` associated with a given element by using its `name`. In this sense, the script's `name`/`value` pairs are quite similar to the key/value pairs of associative arrays.

Text and Password Fields

Our first `<input>` element, as shown in Figure 3.1, is a simple text input field for the user's name:

```
<input type=text name="who">
```

An `<input>` element with the `type` attribute set to `text` displays a single line box into which the user can type an unlimited amount of text. The size of the box on the form and the number of characters allowed in the field can be limited by attributes given with the `<input>` element. Additional attributes give the `name` of the element and an optional default `value`, which is displayed as the initial text in the field. This value is only a default; if the user types something into the field, his or her text will be submitted to the script instead.

A variation on text `<input>` elements are `<input>` elements of type `password`.[4] Password fields are similar to text fields, but they do not display text being entered into them. Despite their name, password fields are not a secure means of entering data because the information in a password field is submitted to a server in the same unencrypted manner as in a text field.[5] Consequently, the password field is useful primarily for applications which require only slightly more privacy than a simple text field would offer.

---

[4] This password field should not be confused with passwords needed to view access-controlled pages. The latter are administered by the server itself, not by the contents of the HTML form.

[5] Forms may be submitted using secure client-server connections such as that provided by the Netscape Commerce Server, in which case this limitation need not apply.

SYNTAX NOTE: `<input>` element, type = text or password

Creates a single-line, text input field.

Attributes:

type = [text|password]. If not specified, defaults to text.

name = identifies this element when it is sent to the script

value = a string that specifies the initial default text displayed in the field.

maxlength = a number which indicates the maximum number of characters allowed in the text input field. If not specified, defaults to unlimited.

size = a number which indicates the width of the displayed field, in characters. This number can be smaller or larger than the maxlength attribute; it affects only the display.

Radio Buttons and Checkboxes

Though checkboxes and radio buttons look nothing at all like text or password fields, they are also created using the `<input>` element. Listing 3.1 shows the source for a checkbox in ***trans.html*** that controls whether to print form parameter information:

```
<input type=checkbox name="params" value=1>
```

Checkboxes, unsurprisingly, are either checked or unchecked. In the example given above, the checkbox element indicates that the browser should send the name params and the value 1 for this element if it is checked when the form is submitted. On the other hand, if the checkbox is unchecked, the script will not receive any information from the params element at all; it might as well not have been on the form.

Radio buttons, such as the ones used in the translator to determine the target language, operate in a similar manner. They, too, have two states, on and off, but like the push-button analog car radios from which they take their name, only one radio button in a bank can be on at any given time.[6] Radio buttons are therefore used to give the user a choice of exactly one option from a list of available choices (see also the `<select>` element). All of the radio buttons that comprise a bank are identified by having the same `name` attribute. Thus, as shown in Listing 3.1, all of the language buttons are given the name `lang` to indicate that they operate as a single unit. Radio buttons report their results to the script in the same way that checkboxes do; the `name` and `value` attributes indicate what information to send for buttons which are checked when the form is submitted. For example, if the user had selected German and submitted the form, the identifier `german` would be sent to the script as the value of the element named `lang`.

Checkboxes and radio buttons can also have a `checked` attribute, which, if present, indicates that the element should be checked by default. Note that since radio buttons are exclusive choices, each bank of buttons should have one (and only one) item which is specified as checked. If no element is specified, the browser is supposed to check the first item in the bank; however, many browsers incorrectly fail to do this, so it's a good idea to make the choice explicit.

One thing worth noting about checkboxes and radio buttons (and in fact all `<input>` elements) is that the `<input>` tag draws only the user interface item itself, not any of its labels or explanatory text.[7] In fact, neither the `name` nor `value` of an element is necessarily related to how it appears on the screen. Instead, ordinary HTML text is used to label and explain the input elements to the user. To illustrate, consider the checkbox on the form shown in Figure 3.1. In the source, the descriptive phrase `"Show form parameters"` is standard HTML text and is not part of the element (it occurs after the closing bracket of the `<input type=checkbox>`). Therefore any explanatory text may use the full capabilities of HTML.

---

[6] The on and off states of a radio button are often also referred to as selected and unselected or, for parallelism with checkboxes, checked and unchecked.

[7] The exceptions to this rule are reset and submit buttons, which are covered later in this chapter.

SYNTAX NOTE: `<input>` element, `type` = `checkbox` or `radio`

Creates a checkbox or radio button.

Attributes:

`type` = [`checkbox`|`radio`]. If not specified, defaults to `text` (see `<input>` type=text).

`name` = identifies this element when it is sent to the script. For radio buttons, all elements in a form with the same `name` will be treated as a bank; when any one of the elements in a bank is checked, the others in the bank will become unchecked.

`value` = an identifier sent to the form if the element is checked when the form is submitted. If a checkbox is unchecked when the form is submitted, neither its name nor its value is sent.

`checked` = if specified, this item is checked by default. For radio buttons, exactly one element per bank should be specified as checked.

The translator form has one additional type of `<input>` element, the `submit` type. Not surprisingly, this creates a *submit button* which, when pressed, sends the form to the script for processing. We'll revisit the submit button towards the end of the chapter.

Scripting

Now that we have created the visual appearance of the form, our next goal is to make sure that any user input gets properly processed. As mentioned earlier, each form has an associated CGI script that handles this very task. When the user presses the submit button on the form, the Web browser encodes the form data and sends it to the server, which then passes the information to the script. Listing 3.2 is the script that processes the form shown earlier in Figure 3.1.

Listing 3.2 The program *trans.cgi* does a lot of work with a little code thanks to the ReadParse function from *cgi-lib.pl*.

```perl
#!/usr/local/bin/perl

require "cgi-lib.pl";

%translateHi = (
    "english", "Hello",
    "french",  "Bonjour",
    "klingon", "nuqneH",
    "spanish", "Hola",
    "japan",   "Konnichiwa"
);

%translateHow = (
    "english", "How are you?",
    "french",  "Comment allez vous?",
    "klingon", "",
    "spanish", "Que tal?",
    "japan",   "Ikagadesuka?"
);

MAIN:
{
    &ReadParse;

    print &PrintHeader;
    print &HtmlTop("Greetings of the world");
    print <<END_OF_TEXT;
<p>Your translation reads:</p>
<blockquote>
$translateHi{$in{'lang'}}, $in{'who'}. $translateHow{$in{'lang'}}
</blockquote>
END_OF_TEXT
```

```
if ($in{'params'}) {
    print "<h2>The CGI form parameters...</h2>\n";
    print &PrintVariables(%in);
}


print &HtmlBot;
}
```

At first glance, this script appears quite similar to the scripts we've seen so far. The familiar `require "cgi-lib.pl"` line starts it off, making all of the library's functions available to ***trans.cgi***. The next section is also similar to our most recent program ***world.cgi***, creating two associative arrays, `%translateHi` and `%translateHow`, that store our translated text.[8] Since the user's name comes in the middle of the phrase we want to translate, we use two arrays—one for the first half of the sentence, which says "Hello," and one for the second half, which asks, "How are you?" Alternatively, we could just as easily have used a single array and inserted the name using one of the text manipulation operators introduced in the previous chapter.

After creating the translation lookup tables as associative arrays, the program starts a `MAIN` program block, the first line of which calls a function we've not yet discussed, `ReadParse`. This simple call holds the key to handling and interpreting all of the HTML form data. `ReadParse`, from the ***cgi-lib.pl*** library, takes care of all of the details of retrieving the form information, parsing and decoding the input stream, and neatly arranging the results in the associative array `%in`. We don't have to know anything about what the CGI information looks like as it's delivered to the form (but we discuss this in Chapter 4). Once `ReadParse` finishes with the form data, the `%in` array contains all of the form data, with the element names (as specified by the `name` attribute in the form) as the index keys and the element values as their values.

---

[8] Apparently, the Klingon language has no use for pleasantries such as "How are you," and therefore the corresponding entry in `%translateHow` is the empty string.

After `ReadParse` has been called, we can treat `%in` like any other associative array, because that's exactly what it is. We can perform a lookup using an element's `name` in order to determine the user's response for that particular item. So, in order to retrieve the user's name from the text field named `who` in Listing 3.1, we could simply look at `$in{'who'}`. Similarly, `$in{'lang'}` contains the value associated with the chosen language. In a rather clever twist, we use the value returned by `$in{'lang'}` as the key into the `%translateHi` and `%translateHow` associative arrays to obtain the proper translations and transmit them to the server (Figure 3.3).

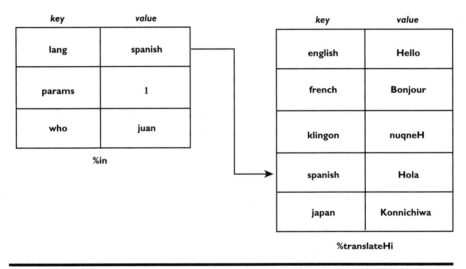

Figure 3.3 The *trans.cgi* script uses the value from one associative array as the key for another.

Occasionally, especially when creating or debugging a new script, it is useful to see all the input that the script receives from the form. The `PrintVariables` function from *cgi-lib.pl* provides this information, iterating through the `%in` associative array and displaying each key and value. In *trans.html*, a checkbox controls whether these variables get displayed. The value of the checkbox is reported to the script by the existence of the `params` element, so the script determines whether to display the variables using the line:

```
if ($in{'params'})
```

If the checkbox were checked, then $in{'params'} would have the value 1. This would be evaluated as true, so the program would call PrintVariables to display the form parameters.[9] If the checkbox were not checked, neither the element's name nor its value would have been sent to the script, and no entry would have been created in the associative array. Since a lookup using a non-existent key is false, the program would skip over the block containing the PrintVariables call and simply go on to print the bottom-of-page tags.

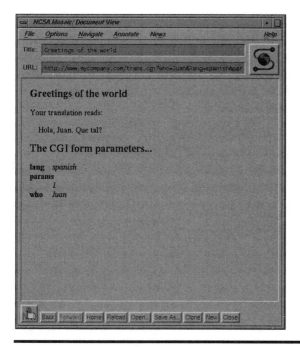

Figure 3.4 The output from **trans.cgi** shows the results of the interactive translator.

---

[9] It is important to note that since the parameter to PrintVariables is the associative array to display, ReadParse must be called first to fill in %in.

Once the script has completed its work and the output winds its way back to the browser, we see something similar to the page shown in Figure 3.4. Thanks in large part to the `ReadParse` function, we can write a script to get at the form data and use it to create this page without really having to know much about CGI at all. The only information we need is the `name` of each `<input>` element that we choose to look up in the associative array `%in`. The program could also have made use of the CGI environment variables, as we demonstrated with ***world.cgi*** in Chapter 2. These variables, stored in the `%ENV` array, are unaffected by the `ReadParse` call.

A <form> Letter

By now, the advantages of using the ***cgi-lib.pl*** library to create CGI scripts are hopefully becoming obvious. The functions in the library do almost all of the work, allowing script writers to concentrate on what the form needs to do, rather than on the "housekeeping" tasks of parsing and interpreting the CGI input. But while the translator script does an adequate job at translating, it could use a number of improvements.

First, the form could certainly be more user friendly. It does no input validation; for example, no error is produced if the user submits the form with a blank input field. Additionally, it would be nice if the "Submit Query" button were more descriptive—"Translate," for instance. More importantly, the two-part nature of the separate form and script opens up the possibility of a number of potential errors.

Because the HTML form is linked to the script by a filename explicitly given in the `action` attribute, ***trans.cgi***, any time we change the name or location of the script, we must remember to update the form. Similarly, if we copy the form to another server, we need to make sure we also copy the script to avoid orphaning the form. Finally, consider what would happen if a user were to go to the address of the script directly:

```
http://www.mycompany.com/trans.cgi
```

A script executed in this way would lack any form information and would become hopelessly confused.

The solution to these problems is to more tightly integrate the form and the script which processes it. We can do this by using a *comboform*. The premise behind a comboform is simple: we have a single script which is called first to display the form and then again in order to process the form data. Listing 3.3 shows a comboform that generates encoded form letters.

Listing 3.3 The Super Encoder, *code.cgi*, is a good example of a comboform, but a poor example of a useful one.

```perl
#!/usr/local/bin/perl


require "cgi-lib.pl";

MAIN:
{
  if (&ReadParse(*input)) {
    &ProcessForm;
  } else {
    &ShowForm;
  }
}


sub ShowForm
{
  print &PrintHeader;
  print &HtmlTop("Super Encoder");
  print <<EOT;
<p>Need to send a secret message to a loved one, but fear that it
will be intercepted and show up in the supermarket tabloids?  This
Super Encoder will solve all your problems.  <b>Note</b>: only the
body of the message is encoded.</p>
```

```
<form method=post>
Select encoding methods:<br>
<ul>
<li><input type=checkbox name=code value=rot13> Rot13
<li><input type=checkbox name=code value=void>  Void
<li><input type=checkbox name=code value=latin> Pig Latin
</ul>
To whom should this be addressed?<br>
<input type=radio name=title value="Dr.">          Dr.
<input type=radio name=title value="Ms.">          Ms.
<input type=radio name=title value="Miss" checked> Miss
<input type=radio name=title value="Mr.">          Mr.
<input type=radio name=title value="Mrs.">         Mrs.

<input type=text name=to value="Manners"><br>

Select one or more phrases:<br>
<select name=phrase size=4 multiple>
<option>Roses are red, violets are blue.
<option>What's your sign?
<option>How do I love thee, let me count the ways.
<option>Objects in mirror are closer than they appear.
<option>Meet me behind the dumpster.
<option>The eagle flies at midnight.
<option>This is only a test.
</select>
<br>

Enter any further comments:<br>
<textarea name=text rows=4 cols=50></textarea>

<br>Choose a closure:
<select name=close>
<option> Love
<option value="Hasta la vista, baby"> Make my day
```

```
<option> Until next we meet
<option selected> Sincerely
<option> Brought to you by the letter 'W'
</select>
<br>

Your name: <input type=text name=from><br>
<input type=submit value="Encode">
<input type=reset value="Reset to defaults">
</form>
EOT

  print &HtmlBot;
}


sub ProcessForm
{
  local (@code, %code, @phrase, $body);

  @code = split("\0", $input{'code'});
  grep($code{$_}++, @code);

  @phrase = split("\0", $input{'phrase'});
  $body = join(" ", @phrase) . " " . $input{'text'};

  $body = &Rot13($body)    if $code{'rot13'};
  $body = &Voidify($body)  if $code{'void'};
  $body = &PigLatin($body) if $code{'latin'};

  print &PrintHeader;
  print &HtmlTop("Your secret text");
  print <<EOT;
<br>Dear $input{'title'} $input{'to'},
<p>$body</p>
<p>$input{'close'},<br>
```

```
<br>
$input{'from'}
EOT
  print &HtmlBot;
}


sub Rot13
{
  local ($text) = @_;
  $text =~ tr/a-mA-Mn-zN-Z/n-zN-Za-mA-M/;
  return $text;
}


sub Voidify
{
  local ($text)= @_;
  local (@words);  # list of all the words, possibly with punctuation

  @words = split(" ", $text);
  grep(s/^[A-Z]\w*/Void/, @words);
  grep(s/^[a-z]\w*/void/, @words);

  return join(" ", @words);
}


sub PigLatin
{
  local ($text) = @_;  # text to be encoded
  local (@words, # list of all the words, possibly with punctuation
         $i,      # loop index
         $word,   # individual word without punctuation
         $punc,   # punctuation following word
         @word,   # individual word as a list of letters
         $pre,    # first part of word (to be moved to end)
         $rest,   # rest of word (after initial consonants)
```

```
        $pig     # the word translated into pig latin
        );

@words = split(" ", $text);
foreach $i (0..$#words) {

    # separate word and punctuation
    ($word, $punc) = ($words[$i] =~ /^(\w*)(.*)$/);

    # does word begin with a vowel?
    if (substr($word,0,1) =~ /[AEIOUaeiou]/) {
      $pig = $word . "yay";
    } else {  # begins with consonant
      ($pre, $rest) = $word =~ /([^AEIOUaeiou]*)(.*)/;
      if (substr($pre,0,1) =~ /[A-Z]/) {    # if first letter is a capital
        substr($rest,0,1) =~ tr/a-z/A-Z/;
        substr($pre, 0,1) =~ tr/A-Z/a-z/;
      }
      $pig = $rest . $pre . "ay";
    }

    $words[$i] = $pig . $punc; # replace original word with coded one
  }

  return join(" ", @words);
}
```

The MAIN block of ***code.cgi*** is quite simple. It consists of a single if statement which calls ShowForm or ProcessForm depending on whether we want to output the HTML form or process the form data. But how does the script know which one of these actions to perform? The answer lies in the return value from ReadParse, which we previously ignored. ReadParse returns true if any form data was passed into the script, and false otherwise. When the user first accesses the script, no form has yet been displayed, so there is obviously no form data. In this instance,

ReadParse returns false, so the script runs the ShowForm subroutine to display the form. Once the user fills in the form and presses the Submit button, **code.cgi** is called a second time, this time with the results from the form. ReadParse then returns true and the script executes the ProcessForm function to generate the appropriate output.

Careful readers will note that **code.cgi** passes a parameter to ReadParse as well. By passing *input[10] into the function, we instruct ReadParse to put all of the form data into the %input array instead of %in. This can be useful in avoiding confusion with other variables named in.

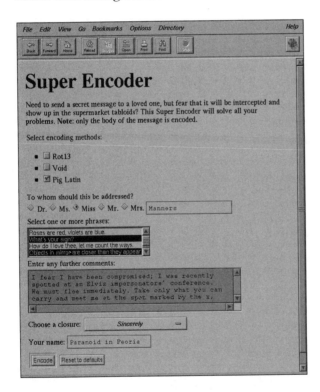

Figure 3.5 The Super Encoder form provides a nice user-interface to simplify the task of writing encoded messages.

---

[10] Variable names beginning with an asterisk are called *type globs*, which represent all the variants of that name. That is, *input represents everything input, including: , $input, @input and %input.

If we take a closer look now at the ShowForm function, we see that it uses essentially the same approach we've seen in previous chapters to generate HTML forms on the fly. The Super Encoder form, shown in Figure 3.5, allows the user to create a suitable message and then encrypt it.

After providing the header information and some introductory text, the page specifies the beginning of the form using the <form> tag. As an attribute to using the <form> tag, we indicate the POST method. Notice, however, that we don't give a script address as the action for the form. If no action attribute is supplied, the form data will be submitted to the form's URL. In other words, the client will believe that the URL for the script is the same as that of the form. This is the case for a comboform, which both displays the form and processes the submitted data. Of course we could have specified the script's address in the <form> element's action attribute, but by omitting the action, we're free to move the script around anywhere on our server without having to update any of the information in the form itself.

As with the translator form, the Super Encoder page goes on to use checkboxes, radio buttons, and text input fields to gather input from the user. Note that we can employ standard HTML, such as the <ul> element, in conjunction with form elements in order to format correctly the page. We also make use of several additional form elements that we haven't previously described.

The <select> and <option> Elements

As its name implies, the <select> element allows users to choose from a list of text items. The Super Encoder form makes use of this element in two places: to help us start by providing a set of stock phrases to begin our note and to select the closing for our letter. We'll start our discussion of <select> with the second of these.

As shown in Figure 3.5, the user can choose the closing for the letter from a pop-up list. This pop-up works like a bank of radio buttons in that only one item may be selected at any given time. However, the pop-up allows for a clearer and more compact visual appearance than the corresponding number of radio buttons.

Unlike radio buttons (or indeed, any of the <input> elements), <select> is a compound element, meaning it has a beginning tag and an ending tag (</select>). The actual items that make up the list are not specified by these tags but are denoted by <option> tags enclosed by the <select> and </select> tags. Because each of these items becomes part of the list, its text may not contain any HTML formatting tags. Each <option> element may take a value attribute that, like the corresponding value attributes for <input> elements, is sent to the script if that element is selected. If an <option> tag lacks a <value> attribute, then the text that follows the <option> tag (i.e., that which is displayed in the form) is sent to the script as that item's value.[11]

The list of stock phrases at the beginning of the form is also constructed using a <select> element. Its appearance is different, however, because the addition of the multiple attribute allows the user to choose multiple items from this list. In almost every respect, multi-select lists behave in the same way as their single-select counterparts. Unfortunately, many browsers do a poor job of presenting an effective interface for multiple selection.

SYNTAX NOTE: <select> element

Creates a list containing one or more items (specified by <option> tags) that the user can choose.

Attributes:

name = a string which identifies this element when it is sent to the script.

multiple = if specified, more than one item can be selected from the list. If absent, only a single item can be chosen.

size = the number of lines of choices displayed in the list. If size is 1, the element will typically be shown as a pop-up menu.

---

[11] Although the default value for an <option> item's value is the text that accompanies the element, some browsers may report a different amount of whitespace for the element's value when it is submitted to a script than is actually given in the text. As a result, scripts which rely on the value being a specific string—for example, those that do string comparisons with the eq operator—should use the value attribute to explicitly indicate an <option> element's value.

SYNTAX NOTE: `<option>` element

Specifies an item in a selection list bracketed by `<select>` and `</select>`. Text following the `<option>` tag is displayed in the `<select>` list.

Attributes:

`value` = the value sent to the script if this item is selected when the form is sent to the browser. If omitted, defaults to the text following the `<option>` tag.

`selected` = if specified, the item is selected by default; more than one `<option>` may be selected if the containing `<select>` block has the `multiple` attribute set.

Multiple-line Text Areas

The last piece of information the Super Encoder needs is any additional text that the user wants to encode. Until now, the only widget which we've seen that allows users to enter text has been the text `<input>` element. But the `<input>` element only allows users to enter a single line of text, and it would be ridiculous to expect our users to compose a full letter in just one line.[12] Clearly, we'd like to have something that could allow a user to enter an arbitrary amount of text as the main body of the message.

The `<textarea>` element fits the bill quite nicely. Like the `<input>` element of type `text` described earlier, `<textarea>` elements accept keyboard input and have a `name` attribute that identifies the element to a script. However, while a text `<input>` is restricted to a single line, a `<textarea>` can show many lines at once; the `rows` and `cols` attributes determine exactly how much text is visible on the screen. If the user types more characters than would fit in the `<textarea>`, the text scrolls vertically and horizontally to accommodate as much text as is entered. Some browsers allow the text to wrap as in a word processor.

---

[12] On the other hand, a form which produces Pig Latin, Rot13, and Void is pretty ridiculous as it stands.

Also different is the way in which `<textarea>` specifies the initial text that will appear in the element. Rather than using a `value` attribute to specify the default text, any text that is given between the `<textarea>` and `</textarea>` tags is used as the initial value. This text can not contain any HTML tags and will not be formatted in any special way.

SYNTAX NOTE: `<textarea>` element

Creates a scrollable field where the user can enter multiple lines of text.

Attributes:

`name` = a string which identifies this element when it is sent to the script.

`rows` = the number of lines of the text field that are visible on the screen.

`cols` = the number of columns of text (as displayed in a fixed-width font) in the text field that are visible on the screen.

`wrap*` = [none|soft|hard] Specifies if word wrap should occur. The `soft` option will wrap the text but report it to the script as a single line, while `hard` will wrap the text and report it as multiple lines. If not specified, the default is `none`, in which case text does not wrap.

Example:

```
<textarea name="inputbox" rows=4 cols=50>
This text will appear as the default in the field.
</textarea>
```

Submit and Reset

Earlier we noted that it would be nice if our submit button could be made more descriptive. For the current form, an appropriate button might be "Encode," which succinctly describes what the form does when submitted. The ability to clear the form and reset all of the elements to their default values would also be useful in the event the user makes a mistake while filling out the form. As Figure 3.5 shows, we've solved both of these problems in the Super Encoder by displaying descriptive text on the face of the submit button and by adding a *reset button*.

As shown in Listing 3.3, both buttons are created using the multi-purpose `<input>` element. The other attributes we can specify for these buttons give us quite a bit of control over their appearance and behavior. Both button types can use the `value` attribute to specify the text that appears on the face of the button. In addition, a submit button can take a `name` attribute to distinguish itself from other submit buttons on the same form. Every form needs at least one submit button[13] of course, but a single form can have multiple submit buttons. The script that is executed when a form is submitted (as well as the `method` and `enctype` used to do so) is specified as an attribute of the `<form>` element and not in the submit button itself. Therefore, every submit button on a page will run the same script. However, because a script can determine which button was used to actually submit the form, having multiple buttons can nonetheless be useful.[14] Consider, for example, a "vote" form. Each submit button could indicate a vote for a particular candidate. The script can then check for the existence of the appropriate `name` in the same way that ***trans.cgi*** checked for the `params` checkbox in Listing 3.2. The Submit buttons that were not used to submit the form will not send any information, nor will the reset button, whose operation is local to the browser.

SYNTAX NOTE: `<input>` element, `type` = `submit` or `reset`

Creates buttons that submit and clear the form.

Attributes:

`type` = [`submit`|`reset`]. If not specified, defaults to `text` (see `<input>` `type` = `text`).

`name` = Not used for Reset buttons. For Submit buttons, a string which identifies this element to the script. Only the `name` (and `value`) of the

---

[13] Or, more specifically, every form needs something that can act as a submit button. An `<input>` element with `type=image` will, when pressed, achieve the same result of packaging the form data and delivering it to the script. This element is described in greater detail later in the chapter.

[14] Note that some browsers do not properly handle forms with multiple submit buttons.

Submit button pressed is sent. If the name attribute is not specified, no `name`/`value` pair is sent.

`value` = a string which specifies the text to be displayed on the button. For submit buttons, this `value` will be sent to the script if a `name` is also specified.

Comboform Processing

After the user finishes filling out the Super Encoder form, he or she presses the "Encode" button in order to send the data to the script for encoding. This time when *code.cgi* is run, the form data will be decoded by `ReadParse` and stored in `%input`. Further, the true return value from `ReadParse` triggers the script to branch to the `ProcessForm` function.

The first thing that `ProcessForm` needs to do is to determine what encryption methods have been requested. We provide three different methods, each of which can be used independently or in conjunction with the others: Pig Latin, Rot13, and Voidify. Many of you may remember Pig Latin from your childhood. It's a silly encoding scheme through which "Scripting the Web is neat" becomes "Iptingscray ethay Ebway isyay eatnay." Rot13, popularized by USENET News, is almost as simple to use, but creates output which is much more difficult to pronounce. Under Rot13, each letter of the alphabet is replaced with the one which comes thirteen letters later, wrapping around from Z to A if necessary. Thus, any occurrence of the letter "B" would be replaced by the letter "O" and vice-versa. Finally, we throw in our own void encoding, in which every word in the text is replaced by "void." This last method is a classic example of a one-way encoding, since once encoded, it is impossible to reverse the process to obtain the original phrase.[15]

---

[15] Normally one-way encoding is used for high-security applications, such as password files, since it is typically difficult to create different sources which produce the same encoded result. Our void encoding doesn't meet this criterion, so it is not terribly useful as a secure encryption system or, for that matter, anything else.

The user can select the desired encryption method(s) using a group of checkboxes. As shown in Listing 3.3, each checkbox is assigned a different value to indicate the encoding type it controls. However, we give them all the same name, `code`, in order to group them together logically and prevent ourselves from having an excessive number of different form parameters.[16] This raises an interesting problem. While the script could be sent up to three different values for the name `code`, an associative array can contain only one value per key. Which value gets stored in the associative array? The answer is: all of them. The ***cgi-lib.pl*** library takes care of this situation by assigning as the value for `code` the concatenation of each of the checkbox values, separated by the ASCII null charachter, represented in Perl as `"\0"`. Thus, if both Rot13 and Pig Latin were specified, `$input{'code'}` would be `"rot13\0latin"`.

Origins of Inscrutability

Convoluted code can be created in almost any computer language, but in some languages, like Perl and C, initially unreadable code is not only tolerated but often encouraged and considered good style. Perhaps the canonical example of this is the C statement:

```
while (*q++ = *p++);
```

Normal human beings will be bewildered by this snippet, but experienced C programmers will immediately recognize it as the "string copy" function, which copies the contents of string p to q. There are three basic reasons why this code might seem confusing:

- There are a lot of things going on, many of them semi-advanced features of the language: pointer dereference, assignment, variable post-increment, boolean evaluation, and repetition.

---

[16] If we didn't care about these factors (you might not), we could have given each checkbox a different name.

- Much of what's actually occurring relies on a number of assumptions: strings are null terminated, satisfactory memory allocation has been done in advance, and a previously defined variable is available in order to access either the original or copied string (since neither p nor q now points to the beginning of the strings). Since we take these assumptions as given, the code does no error checking and is therefore not particularly robust.

- The standard conventions of the language are being subverted: the body of the loop—where most of the action normally occurs—is completely missing. Instead, the boolean test does all the work. Also, the terminating \0 is being used in the slightly unfamiliar context of a boolean value.

Despite all of these pitfalls, however, experienced programmers will write code like this all the time, and there are good reasons for it. This routine is both quick to code and efficient to execute. Furthermore it is *clear*—not because the code is particularly easy to read, but because it is part of the C language idiom. That is, once a programmer learns to "think in C," the assumptions and benefits behind this version of string copy become clear.

Because Perl operates at a higher level than C, it is often possible to write programs that are easier to understand. Perl's analogous string copy would be:

```
$q = $p;
```

This is clear and is even more concise than its C analog, without any of the caveats. However, Perl's higher-level features often simply lead to higher-level obscurities. For example, a routine to count word lengths in Perl will often look something like this:

```
grep($count[length]++, @list);
```

This statement puts its results in the array @count (which is created if it doesn't already exist). The element $count[$n] is the number of occurrences of words of length $n in @list.

This program line is initially confusing for almost exactly the same reasons as C's string copy above: there's a lot going on in a little space, much of the action is unseen, and things aren't happening in the normal way. But once you've learned to "think in Perl," you can begin to understand more of what's going on.

When used for string searching, the `grep` function's first parameter is a pattern to match, and the second is a list to match against. The function returns all of the list entries which match the first parameter. But in this case the return value is completely ignored, and the pattern has been replaced with `$count[length]++`. The secret to understanding this expression is the fact that `grep` really works by iterating through the list, setting the (unseen) special variable `$_` to each list element in turn, then running the pattern match (or other expression) on `$_`. So, if we forget about the return value and some other subtleties, the code could be re-written as:

```
for ($i = 0; $i <= $#list; $i++) {
  $_ = $list[$i];
  $count[length]++;
}
```

This code still leaves a bit unseen, because the `length` function (like many others) automagically operates on the `$_` variable if none is given. Therefore the index to `$count[]` will be set to the length of the current element of `@list`. The `++` increments the value of the `$count[length]` element by one; this gives the correct result because Perl initializes the value of every element to zero.

As in our example, the `grep` function is probably used more often for its side effects than for its original intended use, so it's helpful to be on the lookout for those applications. Of course, not all Perl code will be as convoluted as this, but don't be surprised to find that as you become more familiar with Perl, your own code begins to look less obvious. However, this should be no cause for alarm. By using established idioms, it will immediately be understandable by other Perl experts.

This concatenated form is not a terribly convenient format for this information, so we use the `split` function which, true to its name, splits a string into an array of strings. We give `split` the pattern which delimits each item in the string, `"\0"`, and the string to pull apart, in this case `$input{'code'}`. In our earlier example, the resulting array, `@code`, would contain the elements `rot13` and `latin`.

This array is much nicer than a single string, but it's still not the optimal way to look up which encryptions we need to perform. To make this information easier to digest, we turn to the `grep` function. We don't use the `grep` function as a search operator (its nominal purpose). Indeed, unless you know Perl well, our actual usage is virtually indecipherable:

```
grep($code{$_}++, @code);
```

If you are "thinking in Perl", this usage is immediately obvious. If not, don't worry too much; this is another of those funny Perlisms that can be so useful. We'll start off by first explaining what this statement does and then go back to show how it actually does it. In order to determine quickly which encoding schemes the user requested, we want to create an associative array `%code`, in which the keys are the encoding schemes—`rot13`, `void`, and `latin`—and the values are true if the user requests that encoding, false if not. Then the script could simply check the value of `$code{'rot13'}`, for example, to determine if the user requested Rot13 encoding.

The method used to accomplish this task actually relies on a side effect of how `grep` goes about its work. Normally, `grep` is used to find occurrences of a pattern (its first parameter) within a list (its second). To do this, `grep` iterates through each item in the list and evaluates the expression in the first parameter. Each time through the iteration, `grep` assigns the list item it is currently working on to the magic variable `$_`. Therefore, when `grep` first evaluates the expression `$code{$_}` in our example, `$_` would be `rot13` (since `split` created `@code` with `rot13` and `latin`). Accordingly, the actual expression on the left is effectively the same as $code{'rot13'}++. Finally, because all Perl variables are initialized to zero, the increment operator (++) sets the value to one.[17]

Now that it knows how to encode the text, the script needs to actually retrieve the text to encode. The message text consists of the items the user chose from the list of standard phrases, followed by any text that he or she typed into the <textarea>.

Let's start with the list of phrases. The ***cgi-lib.pl*** library reports the selected values in a multiple select using the same procedure as it does for multiple checkboxes with the same name. That is, each of the selected items is concatenated into a single string, separated by "\0" characters. We can therefore use split to first separate the phrases into an array of strings, then rejoin them with spaces using the join function:

```
@phrase = split("\0", $input{'phrase'});
$body = join(" ", @phrase);  # we omit the text concatenate here
```

As you might expect, in the classic Perl tradition, we could have accomplished this task in any number of ways. One alternative, for example, would have been to use the substitution operator s/// introduced in Chapter 2 to simply substitute spaces for "\0" characters:

```
$input{'phrase'} =~ s/\0/ /g;
```

Once we have all of the phrases in the $body variable, we append the text from the <textarea>, which is simply a normal associative array element. As you may recall from earlier, the dot (.) operator concatenates strings together, so when we're through with the munging, $body contains the entire message text that we want to encode.

Having already determined what kind of encoding is needed, the next three lines simply call functions to do it. The order of these statements is important. The text is first encrypted into Rot13, if desired, and the resultant message is then voidified. Finally, the void output is encoded in Pig Latin. Each of these lines makes use of a variant of the if statement to

---

[17] This code could perhaps be made a tiny bit easier by changing the left hand side to $code{$_}=1. For that matter, we could replace the entire grep with the following:
```
foreach $encoding (@code) { $code{$encoding}=1; }
```
However, the statement we give in the text is more a part of the Perl idiom.

determine whether to perform the encoding. The operation on the left is performed only if the expression on the right evaluates to true.

We won't go into how the encoders actually work, because they have little to do with CGI. If you look through the code, however, you might want to be aware of some of their strong and weak points. In general, they preserve capitalization, although words in all capitals would confuse them. The encoders also try to retain punctuation but don't preserve whitespace exactly. Along the way, they show off some interesting Perlisms, most of which look like gibberish to the untrained eye.

After having run all of the body text through the appropriate encoders, all that remains is to send the results off to the browser for display. We do this in the standard way, by printing a here document. When displayed on a Web browser, it yields the page shown in Figure 3.6.

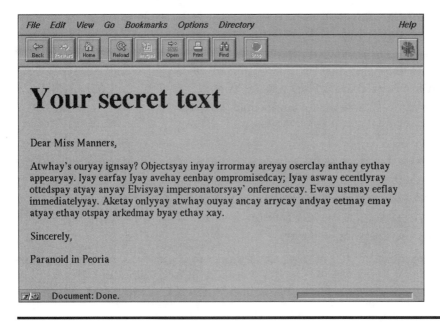

Figure 3.6 Our Super Encoder allows you to create text so completely encrypted that even you won't know what you wrote.

But Wait, There's More!

There are a few form elements that didn't make their way into our examples but are quite useful nonetheless. Each is a variant of the `<input>` element, but they share little in common with each other or with the other elements we've explored in this chapter.

Images

Clickable image maps have been in use on the Web for some time, allowing users to retrieve a new page by clicking on a portion of an inlined image. Over time, a number of ways to implement these image maps have been developed. One of the most flexible methods came with the introduction of HTML forms. An `<input>` element with the `type` attribute set to `image` creates a clickable image. The `src` and `align` attributes, respectively, give the URL of the image and indicate how it should be aligned on the page.

Like other `<input>` elements, clickable images also have a `name` attribute, but the `image` type is unique in two important ways. First, clicking on an image element immediately submits the form, packaging the data and delivering it to the script for processing just as though the image were a submit button. Second, each image element sends *two* name/value pairs to the form. The names are given as `.x` and `.y` appended to the `name` attribute, and their values are the *x* and *y* coordinates where the mouse was clicked (relative to the top-left corner of the image). Thus, if the image's `name` attribute were `iconbar`, the pointer location would be passed to the script as the names `iconbar.x` and `iconbar.y`. Typically, the script reads these values and, based on some knowledge of the image, instructs the client to jump to another page. Redirection of this sort is described in greater detail in Chapter 4.

SYNTAX NOTE: `<input>` element, `type = image`

Creates a clickable image that submits the form.

Attributes:

`type = image`. If not specified, defaults to `text`
  (see `<input>` `type = text`).

`name` = identifies this element when it is sent to the script. The actual
  names sent to the script will be constructed by appending `.x` and `.y` to
  this name.

`src` = the URL of an image to display.

`align` = [top|middle|bottom]. Specifies the alignment of the image on
  the line. If not specified, defaults to bottom.

Example:

```
<input type=image name="iconbar" align=middle
  src="http://www.mycompany.com/iconbar.gif">
```

File Upload*

Although not yet widely implemented and not officially part of any HTML
standard, the `<input>` element of type `file` could prove to be quite
useful.[18] The file `<input>` element allows users to transmit the contents
of a file directly from within an HTML form. You might imagine the Super
Encoder as a Web service that could receive a user's file, encode it, and
then display the output to the user. Any number of such services could be
implemented, each accepting files directly and therefore saving the user
from repetitive typing. This also allows users to easily submit files
containing information which is difficult to directly input from a keyboard,
such as images.

Conceptually, the file `<input>` element is quite simple. It accepts a
`name` attribute like all other `<input>` elements, and displays an interface
from which the user can choose a single file to send. Unfortunately, the

---

[18] A pointer to the full specification for file uploads (RFC 1867) is available online; see Appendix D,
Online Resources.

complexities involved in actually sending the data require an entirely new encoding scheme to handle files. Accordingly, in order to use this type of `<input>` element, the `<form>` element in which it is contained must be submitted using `method=POST` and `enctype=multipart/form-data`. This latter attribute indicates that the information is sent to the script as a multipart Media Type, which is somewhat more complicated than the `application/x-www-form-urlencoded` type in widespread practice today. However, for *cgi-lib.pl* users, the change is less important, since `ReadParse` will take care of parsing the data stream and filling the `%in` associative array correctly, regardless of the encoding scheme in use.

SYNTAX NOTE: `<input>` element, `type = file`

Creates an element that allows a file to be attached to a form.

Attributes:

`type = file`. If not specified, defaults to `text`
  (see `<input> type = text`).

`name` = identifies this element when it is sent to the script.

`accept` = a list of Media Types that are acceptable to upload.If not
  specified, a file of any type may be selected.

Example:
`<input type=file name=userdata>`

Hidden Elements

At first glance, a form element that doesn't display anything to the user might seem rather useless. But it turns out that there are some very good reasons to have an `<input>` element which accepts no user input. Hidden elements circumvent the fact that HTTP is a stateless protocol, and they allow state information—data that is remembered from a previous interaction—to be tucked away as part of a form, unseen by the user.

The "shopping bags" that are prevalent on many Internet shopping sites can be implemented quite easily with hidden elements. Each product description is actually a form which contains information about the product, as well as hidden elements which store the items collected in the shopping bag so far. If the user submits the form to "add" an item to the bag, the processing script adds it as a hidden element to the next page displayed, along with all of the previously chosen products. When it comes time to process the order, the hidden elements on the order form contain all of the requested items.

The syntax of a hidden element is quite simple. It takes two attributes, the name and the value, which are simply passed to the script when the form is submitted.

SYNTAX NOTE: `<input>` element, `type = hidden`

Creates an element that stores data but is not visible to the user.

Attributes:

`type` = `hidden`. If not specified, defaults to `text`
  (see `<input>` `type = text`).

`name` = identifies this element when it is sent to the script.

`value` = the value sent to the script when the form is submitted.

Example:
```
<input type=hidden name=bag value="apples">
<input type=hidden name=bag value="oranges">
```

Next Steps

By combining the many different types of form elements with the power of CGI scripts written in Perl, it is possible to create a vast array of interactive Web systems. However, the wealth of possibilities they present might at first seem overwhelming. Our advice is to start off with small, manageable projects and build up to increasingly complicated ones. This evolutionary approach makes sense for HTML forms because each component can be considered as an independent module of a more integrated whole.[19] Consider what we might do, for instance, to make the translation form and script shown at the beginning of this chapter more sophisticated.

To start, we could combine the working form and script into a comboform. This simple exercise provides immediate benefits and also provides a stepping stone for future enhancements. As we've discussed, a comboform prevents the form page from becoming separated from its processing script. More interestingly, once unified, we can take advantage of a number of Perl features to make them work better together. For example, rather than statically producing a bank of radio buttons that allow the user to choose a language, Perl code can be used to dynamically generate HTML. Thus, the script could determine which languages to include on the form by interating through the keys of the translation table associative arrays. Then, if a new language (and translation) were added to the tables, the script would automatically create a corresponding option.

Further, we could make our ***hey.cgi*** script part of a more complicated translation system, with multiple forms used in succession. By using hidden <input> elements, each form could include state information. Thus, information like the user's name, which doesn't change, can be gathered once and then passed to each subsequent form for processing. We could continue in this vein, using the dynamic nature of scripts to add more features or to reduce the work involved in maintaining a complex Web site. But whether your plans call for an elaborate translation system or just a form for amusement, the fundamentals of processing forms with CGI scripts remain the same.

---

[19] In a traditional programming model, it's preferable to start with a complete design rather than with scattered pieces. Web applications, however, often lend themselves to creeping featurism.

Review: Scripting with Forms

As we've seen in this chapter, creating interactive forms isn't hard. The two examples we presented took us on a whirlwind tour of many of the HTML form elements and ***cgi-lib.pl*** functions that will be common to most applications of interactive forms. And even without learning too much about CGI, it is possible to develop applications which are able to really take advantage of the Web's interactive, dynamic nature. Some of the more important aspects of creating interactive forms are:

- Forms are simply HTML pages that make use of special tags to provide an interface to solicit information from the user. Each form relies on a script to process the results.

- The `<form>` tag sets apart a logical form and establishes the relationship between the form and the CGI script that processes its data.

- A number of form elements, including `<input>`, `<select>`, and `<textarea>`, can be employed to create the user interface for the form. These are summarized in Table 3.1, below.

- Each form element has both a `name` and a `value`, which the script receives when the form is submitted.

- The `ReadParse` function, from ***cgi-lib.pl***, does all of the work of parsing the form results and placing them into an associative array, `%in`. Each HTML element's `name` and `value` are converted to a corresponding key and value of the associative array `%in`. The `PrintVariables` function provides a convenient way to look at all of the form data that is given as input to the script.

- Comboforms unify form generation and processing into a single script, thus obviating a wide variety of problems. Comboforms rely on the fact that `ReadParse` returns a true value only if there is form data; if there is no such data, it returns a false value.

Table 3.1 HTML Form Element Summary

To display:	Use:	Attributes:

A form	`<form>`
	 ... HTML form info
	 `</form>`
		`method` - `GET` or `POST` - how to submit data
		 `action` - URL or filename of script
		 `enctype` - `application/x-www-form-urlencoded`
		 or `multipart/form-data`*

Single-line text field	`<input type=text>`	`name` - identifies the element `value` - default text `maxlength` - max # of chars in field `size` - size of visible field
Single-line password field	`<input type=password>`	`name` - identifies the element `value` - default text `maxlength` - max # of chars in field `size` - size of the visible field

Multiple-line text area	`<textarea>`
	 default text
	 `</textarea>`
		`name` - identifies the element
		 `rows` - # of rows of text to display
		 `cols` - # of columns of text to display
		 `wrap`* - none|soft|hard - word wrap

Checkbox	`<input type=checkbox>`	`name` - identifies the element `value` - submitted to the script only if checked `checked` - if present, element is checked by default
Radio buttons	`<input type=radio>`	`name` - identifies the element and also groups buttons together in a bank `value` - submitted to the script only if checked `checked` - if present, element is checked by default

List of choices	`<select>`
	 One or more `<option>` elements
	 `</select>`
		`name` - identifies the element
		 `multiple` - if present, user can select multiple items
		
		 `size` - number of choices displayed

Items in a `<select>` list	`<option>`	`value` - submitted to the script if this option is selected `selected` - if present, element is selected by default
Clickable image	`<input type=image>`	`name` - `.x` and `.y` are added to create two names, both of which are submitted to the script. `align` -top|middle|bottom `src` - a URL to an image
File upload *†	`<input type=file>`	`name` - identifies the element `accept` - a list of Media Types

Table 3.1   HTML Form Element Summary (continued)

To display:	Use:	Attributes:
Hidden field	`<input type=hidden>`	`name` - identifies the element
		`value` - submitted to the script
Reset button	`<input type=reset>`	`value` - label for the button
Submit button	`<input type=submit>`	`name` - if specified, identifies the the pressed button to the scripts.
		`value` - provides a label for the button. If `name` is present and this button is pressed, this `value` is submitted to the script.

* Not part of HTML 2.0

† Requires form `enctype` to be `multipart/form-data` and `method` to be `POST`.

## CHAPTER 4

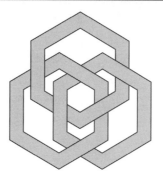

Controlling the Communication with HTTP and CGI

The Hypertext Transport Protocol (HTTP) and Common Gateway Interface (CGI) are the protocols that govern interactions between client, server, and script. Although quite simple, they are flexible enough to perform even unusual tasks. Thanks to the widespread availability of Web tools and scripting aids such as *cgi-lib.pl*, few users will need to know any details of these protocols' operation. Nonetheless, those who want to do something that is a little out of the ordinary or who wish to have greater control over the interaction will find a basic understanding of these protocols to be useful.

This chapter is not intended to be an exhaustive reference to HTTP and CGI but instead focuses on aspects of the protocol that may be of potential interest to script authors. The Online Appendix (see Appendix D) has pointers to more complete information, including current standards documents.

The Hypertext Transport Protocol

The Hypertext Transport Protocol (HTTP) is the principal means by which a Web server and a client communicate with each other. Under this protocol, a client[1] sends a *request* to the server to retrieve a document or execute a script. The server complies and sends back a *response* containing the requested output or an error message if something went wrong. Together, the request and response form a *transaction*—a single interaction between server and client. As a user navigates through a Web site, a number of these transactions are initiated by the browser on his or her behalf, but each transaction is independent of all the rest; a given transaction doesn't make any assumptions about those that preceded it or the ones that will follow.[2]

Both the request and response are sent as ASCII text, which makes it quite easy to see exactly what they are doing. The sections which follow show what happens when a client asks a server for a static document at the URL:

```
http://www.mycompany.com/docs/hello.html
```

This is the same transaction shown in Chapter 1 and represented graphically in Figure 1.2b. Here, we focus on the details of the HTTP communication.

The HTTP Request

A request is nothing more than a message sent from a client to a server. It consists of a single request line, optionally followed by any number of header lines. A mandatory blank line signals the end of the headers, after which the client may send a message body. A request for the "Hello

---

[1] Clients generally are Web browsers, but Web search engines, "robots," and "spiders" also use HTTP to gather information from servers.

[2] Technically, this means that the protocol is *stateless*.

world" page, sent once the client machine had connected to the server at www.mycompany.com, would look something like Listing 4.1.

Listing 4.1 A simple request. The header information shown is followed by a blank line; this particular request has no message body.

```
GET /docs/hello.html HTTP/1.0
Referer: http://www.mycompany.com/docs/index.html
User-Agent: Mozilla/1.22 (Windows; I; 32bit)
Accept: */*
Accept: image/gif
Accept: image/x-xbitmap
Accept: image/jpeg
```

The syntax of the request line (the first line) is quite straightforward. The GET specifies the *method* of the request, which determines how additional information is sent to the server. The method is followed by the name of the resource requested. Note that this isn't a complete URL; the machine name is omitted, since the browser has already made a connection to the desired server. The final portion specifies the version of the protocol in use, namely HTTP1.0.

The headers that accompany an HTTP request, summarized in Table 4.2 (at the end of this chapter), convey additional information about the connection. The Referer (sic) header indicates the page which contains the hyperlink used to access **hello.html**, while User-agent specifies the name and version of the client software.[3] The Accept headers indicate what Media Types the client can properly process; this client indicates that it can handle any type by specifying */*.

Messages sent using the POST method (described later in this chapter) have additional headers that provide information about the message body, such as its length and Media Type. The table at the end of this chapter

---

[3] Netscape clients identify themselves as the Netscape mascot, Mozilla.

describes a few additional header lines, but most of these are used only in specific circumstances and are not sent as part of a typical request.

Executing the request is remarkably simple. In fact, since HTTP requests are sent as plain text, you can enter a request yourself just by using `telnet` to connect to the HTTP port of your favorite Web server (typically port 80):

```
telnet www.mycompany.com 80
```

Once connected, simply type the following request line and press the Enter key twice to obtain the top level page:

```
GET / HTTP/1.0
```

At this point, your screen is likely to be swamped with the HTML of the page whose address is `http://www.mycompany.com/`. The server will then close the connection. This is the server's response.

The HTTP Response

The HTTP response consists of a status line which, like the HTTP request, is then followed by several header lines, a blank line, and possibly a message body. Listing 4.2 shows the response we might receive to the "Hello World" request, given earlier as Listing 4.1.

The first line of the server response begins with a protocol identifier, indicating that the response conforms to HTTP version 1.0. This is followed by a status code which, in this example, informs the client that the request was successful. The headers that follow indicate the date and time of the reply and the type of server in use. They also provide information about the body, namely its `Content-type` and length (in bytes), as well as the time at which it was last changed. A blank line separates the headers from the body of the message—which in this case is the HTML text of ***hello.html***.

Listing 4.2 A simple HTTP response.

```
HTTP/1.0 200 Document follows
Date: Thu, 07 Oct 1971 22:12:15 GMT
Server: NCSA/1.4.2
Content-type: text/html
Last-modified: Sun, 27 Jun 1971 22:17:00 GMT
Content-length: 129

<html>
<head>
<title>Hello world!</title>
</head>
<body>
<h1>Hello world!</h1>
<p>Greetings and salutations.</p>
</body>
</html>
```

Script Input

From the browser's point of view, fetching a document and executing a script are nearly identical operations. As discussed in Chapter 1, an HTTP GET request can be employed to perform either task; the primary differences occur on the server side. However, when running a script, the browser may need to convey additional information, such as the user's input from a form, to the script. Here, we turn our attention to how the browser delivers such information to the server, as well as the details of how the server forwards the data to a script.

There are three fundamental ways in which a client can send additional information to a server: by supplying extra path information, by using extended URLs with query strings, and by using the POST method to submit a message body as part of the request. The manner in which the information is delivered to the server over HTTP determines how the server will pass the data on to the script via CGI.

Extra Path

Extra path information provides a simple means of sending parameters to a script. In this approach, additional information is simply appended to the end of the URL used to access the script. For example, consider a simple address lookup program implemented using a CGI script. The script itself might be available at the URL:

```
http://www.mycompany.com/getaddr.cgi
```

A name could be retrieved from the address book by simply specifying extra path information:

```
http://www.mycompany.com/getaddr.cgi/john/smith
```

To the client, the complete URL—including the extra path information— looks completely normal; the client can't tell that /john/smith is not part of the address of the file. Since URLs are usually encoded by clients to protect spaces and other special characters from being misinterpreted or garbled, extra path information will also be encoded.

When the server receives a request for this address, it determines that the script name is ***getaddr.cgi*** and that the remaining parts of the address must therefore be extra path information. Accordingly, the server executes the script and places the additional information in the environment variable PATH_INFO. A Perl CGI script could then access the data by using the expression:

```
$ENV{'PATH_INFO'}
```

Unfortunately, since there is no way for the client to dynamically create extra path addresses, specifying parameters through this sort of URL is of limited utility. In the address book example, it would be necessary to have a hyperlink for each entry:

```
<a href="http://www.mycompany.com/getaddr.cgi/mary/doe"> Mary Doe</a>
<a href="http://www.mycompany.com/getaddr.cgi/bill/lee"> Bill Lee</a>
<a href="http://www.mycompany.com/getaddr.cgi/john/smith"> John Smith</a>
...etc.
```

Alternately, the user would have to type in the address with the information appended. For this reason, extra path information is now rarely used; most script writers instead opt to use one of the more flexible approaches.

Extended URLs and Query Strings

Extended URLs with query information also specify additional data at the end of the script's address. Unlike extra-path addresses, however, a question mark is used to divide the name of the script to be executed from the additional data, called the *query string*.[4] Isindex pages use this approach, simply appending the user's input to the end of the URL (see sidebar). As with extra path information, the query string is encoded (for example, spaces are converted to plus signs) in order to prevent confusion with actual address information. Thus, an isindex query for the address book page might look like:

```
http://www.mycompany.com/addridx.cgi?John+Smith
```

When the server receives this query, it executes the named script, placing the information beyond the question mark in the CGI environment variable QUERY_STRING. Because the data comes from an isindex query, it is also decoded and placed on the program's command line.

---

[4] It is possible to combine extra path and query information, as in:

```
http://www.mycompany.com/addridx.cgi/name?John+Q.+Smith
```

Here the /name is extra path information, indicating that this is a lookup-by-name, while John+Q.+Smith is the encoded query string.

Using Isindex Pages

Prior to the introduction of forms, isindex pages were the only means of retrieving textual input from World Wide Web users. The inclusion of an `<isindex>` element on a page signals the browser to display a text box in which a user can type query information. Since the browser can only display one box per page, each page can have only one `<isindex>` tag. The actual field resembles the form `<input>` element of type `text` and allows the user to enter a single line of information.

As with a comboform, a single script is responsible both for displaying the HTML page (with the `<isindex>` element) and processing the data. The first time the script is called, the absence of query data causes the script to return the HTML to construct the page with the `<isindex>` element. The browser displays the page and creates both a query input box and a submission button. After the user has filled in the query and submitted the request, the browser delivers the query data to the server, which forwards it on to the script. The request is a standard HTTP `GET` request, with a question mark and an encoded version of the user's query string appended to the URL of the current page. To give a concrete example, suppose the isindex page were located at:

```
http://www.mycompany.com/isindex.cgi
```

Then, a query consisting of the word "tiger" would be formulated into a request for:

```
http://www.mycompany.com/isindex.cgi?tiger
```

When the server receives the request, it decodes the information and launches the script, passing it the decoded query string as command line arguments. Accordingly, the script need not use `ReadParse`, but should instead inspect the special Perl variable `@ARGV`, which contains a program's command line arguments.

Though the HTML 2.0 draft standard continues to support `<isindex>` within a document's `<head>` element, HTML forms offer a much more flexible and superior approach.

Forms which use the GET method also submit their data as part of the URL. The data is sent as a series of name=value pairs, separated by ampersands. Listing 4.3 shows a forms-based version of the address book.

Listing 4.3 The *addrform.html* form is an interface to a Web address book. It sends its results to the *addrform.cgi* script using GET.

```
<html>
<head>
<title>Address Book</title>
</head>
<body>
<h1>Address Book</h1>
<p>Search for a name:</p>

<form method=GET action="http://www.mycompany.com/addrform.cgi">
<br>First Name: <input type=text name=first>
<br>Last Name: <input type=text name=last>
<br><input type=submit>
</form>
</body>
</html>
```

If "John Smith" were entered in this form, the client would generate the following URL:

```
http://www.mycompany.com/addrform.cgi?first=John&last=Smith
```

As in the isindex case, the question mark demarcates the boundary between the name of the script, *addrform.cgi*, and the query information. The server parses this address and runs *addrform.cgi*, providing first=John&last=Smith in the QUERY_STRING environment variable.

Ordinary hyperlinks may also specify URLs which include a query string. This makes it possible to create hyperlinks whose action is equivalent to a user's filling out a form:

```
<a href="http://www.mycompany.com/addrform.cgi?first=John&amp;last=Smith">
John Smith's address</a>
```

To the address book script, input from a user's click on this hyperlink would be essentially indistinguishable from data which was manually entered into the form and submitted. Note that when this URL is placed in HTML, the ampersands must be escaped as &,[5] since the ampersand symbol has special meaning in HTML text.

The POST Method

The POST method uses the message body to send additional information from the user, rather than encoding it as part of the URL.[6] If the form in Listing 4.3 specified method=POST, the client's HTTP request would look similar to the one shown in Listing 4.4.

The client can send anything in the body, as long as the server (and script) can understand it. File uploads (forms with <input type=file> elements), for example, use the recently introduced encoding called multipart/form-data. This looks completely different from the ampersand-delimited name/value pairs used with the more common application/x-www-form-urlencoded encoding type.

---

[5] Alternatively, we could have used semicolons (;) in place of ampersands. These are also recognized as separators between name/value pairs.

[6] It is valid to combine extra path information and POST, just as one could combine extra path and GET. Many servers also support combining query strings with POST requests, but we don't recommend this practice. In order to send information to a script without displaying it to the user, we instead suggest using the <input type=hidden> element described in Chapter 3.

Listing 4.4 Input for scripts called using the POST method is made available in the body of the message.

```
POST /cgi-bin/addrform.cgi HTTP/1.0
Referer: http://www.mycompany.com/docs/index.html
User-Agent: Mozilla/1.22 (Windows; I; 32bit)
Accept: */*
Accept: image/gif
Accept: image/x-xbitmap
Accept: image/jpeg
Content-type: application/x-www-form-urlencoded
Content-length: 21


first=John&last=Smith
```

The HEAD Method

The HTTP/1.0 specification defines one additional request method: HEAD. The HEAD method works similarly to the GET method, except that the response consists solely of the HTTP response headers (hence the name) that would have accompanied the requested resource. This can be useful to determine if a file exists or has been updated, without the transfer of large amounts of data. The HEAD request method is generally not useful for CGI scripts.

GET vs. POST

The GET and POST methods both deliver information to a script, but because they do so in different ways, there are some reasons why you might choose to use one method rather than the other. According to the HTTP specification, GET should be used for operations which don't change the state of the server; that is, simple document retrieval, database lookup, and the like.[7] By contrast, the POST method is recommended

---

[7] The HTTP specification refers to these types of actions as *idempotent*—a word which isn't in our dictionaries, either.

when the operation might alter the server's data. The POST method would therefore be appropriate for adding records to a database, posting to a newsgroup, or changing some server setting.

In practice, however, these distinctions take a back seat to more practical concerns. On some systems, environment variables such as QUERY_STRING are subject to restrictions on length. Therefore, scripts which process a lot of data (those with <textarea> fields for example) may be unable to access all of it. This is the reason why forms that use the multipart/form-data encoding, which can generate extremely long messages, must use the POST method.

Another issue to consider is that the GET method places all of the entered form data in the URL, while POST hides it from the user.[8] Hiding data can be useful in making the script appear cleaner, but it leads to additional problems if form and script become separated. Saving the URL of a script called using GET (in a hotlist, for instance) will include all the information needed to regenerate the appropriate output, because the URL contains the encoded form data. On the other hand, a saved URL for a script called using POST would contain no data; if the script were not a comboform capable of generating the form (or at least an error message), erroneous output could be produced.

Finally, though most modern clients and servers are equally adept at handling both GET and POST methods, GET is the more widely supported of the two. Whichever method you ultimately choose, *cgi-lib.pl* will present the data to your script in the same way.

CGI Environment Variables

CGI specifies that scripts receive input from the server in the form of environment variables, in addition to that information originally provided by the client. One of these variables was used by the ***world.cgi*** script in Chapter 2 to determine the client machine's location. Recall that in Perl, environment variables are accessible as elements of the associative array %ENV. The environment variables defined by CGI are:

---

[8] Though it is not difficult for a user to determine the data from a POST request, if desired.

- AUTH_TYPE: The name of the authentication method used to identify and validate the user. This is only set if the server supports authentication and if the script is protected.

- CONTENT_LENGTH: The number of bytes of information passed to the script via standard input. It is only valid with scripts called using POST. Note that script input is not terminated with a newline or end of file, so it is crucial that scripts use this information to read only the correct number of bytes.

- CONTENT_TYPE: The Media Type of any data provided to the script via standard input. It is valid only with scripts called using POST. In conjunction with CONTENT_LENGTH, this variable provides the information necessary to correctly parse the client's data. Most POST scripts will be called with a CONTENT_TYPE of application/x-www-form-urlencoded.

- GATEWAY_INTERFACE: The name and revision of the protocol being used by the server to communicate with the script. For CGI programs, this will take the form of: CGI/revision. At the time of this writing, the CGI revision level is 1.1.

- PATH_INFO: Any extra path information specified in the URL that accessed this script. As noted earlier in the Extra Path section, the extra path could be used to specify additional parameters that govern a script's operation.

- PATH_TRANSLATED: The server computer's absolute filesystem path to the location of the script. This information is necessary because the root of a URL that identifies a script (as specified in the SCRIPT_NAME environment variable) is usually not the same as the root of the filesystem.

Thus, if the HTTP server at www.mycompany.com had its document root set as:

```
/usr/local/etc/httpd/htdocs
```

then a URL which accesses the document at:

```
http://www.mycompany.com/cheers.html
```

would in fact be getting the document:

```
/usr/local/etc/httpd/htdocs/cheers.html
```

on the machine specified by www.mycompany.com. This information is especially important for scripts, since a script may need to read data or configuration files that are stored in the script's directory. Thus, a call to a script addressed as:

```
http://www.mycompany.com/cgi-bin/world.cgi
```

might have its PATH_TRANSLATED variable set to:

```
/usr/local/etc/httpd/cgi-bin/world.cgi
```

Any extra path information specified in the address is also appended to PATH_TRANSLATED.

- QUERY_STRING: Any additional information passed to the script after a question mark. This variable will contain parameter information from isindex queries and forms submitted with method GET. See the Extended URLs and Query Strings section earlier in this chapter for more information on QUERY_STRING.

- REMOTE_ADDR: The IP address of the client machine making the request.

- REMOTE_HOST: The Fully Qualified Domain Name of the client machine making the request. If the host name cannot be determined, the REMOTE_ADDR variable will contain the IP address of the host and this variable will not be set.

- REMOTE_IDENT: The client machine's username for the user making this request (if available). Servers are usually not able to obtain remote users' names, so this field is generally not available to scripts.

- REMOTE_USER: The name used to authenticate the user and allow access to the script. This is only set if the server supports authentication and the script is protected by some authentication method, as indicated by AUTH_TYPE. It bears no direct relationship to REMOTE_IDENT.

- REQUEST_METHOD: The request method that was used: either GET or POST. Script writers can use this environment variable to determine how the server provides information to the script. Parameters for scripts called using the GET method are made available in the environment variable QUERY_STRING or on the command line, whereas those made using method POST send data to the script's standard input.

- SCRIPT_NAME: The virtual name (i.e., the URL without the protocol identifier, machine name, or port number) of the script being executed, with extra path information stripped out. Multipart forms and comboforms can use this variable to create self-references that will be correct no matter where the script is located on the server. In order to assemble the full URL, it is necessary to combine data from the SERVER_NAME, SERVER_PORT and SCRIPT_NAME variables. In Perl, this would look like:

```
http://$ENV{'SERVER_NAME'}:$ENV{'SERVER_PORT'}$ENV{'SCRIPT_NAME'}
```

- SERVER_NAME: The server name, Fully Qualified Domain Name (if available), or IP address of the server answering the request.

- SERVER_PORT: The port number on the server to which the request was sent. The default port for HTTP requests is 80.

- SERVER_PROTOCOL: The name and revision of the protocol this request uses, in the form protocol/revision. For most current Web applications, this will be HTTP/1.0.

- SERVER_SOFTWARE: This environment variable identifies the name and revision level of the HTTP server that is communicating with the script. This is sent in the form name/version.

Additionally, CGI specifies that the server should pass along to the script any additional information available from HTTP headers sent with the client's request (See Table 4.2). This information is given in environment variables whose names begin with HTTP_. The remainder of the name is derived from the HTTP header name, with dashes changed to underscores and all characters converted to uppercase. Among the most useful of these header lines are the User-agent, Referer, and Accept fields:

- HTTP_ACCEPT: Gives a comma-separated list of MIME types that the client can accept. For text-only browsers, for example, this may consist only of:

  `text/html, text/plain`

  whereas graphical browsers might be capable of handling additional types:

  `text/html, text/plain, image/gif, image/jpeg`

- HTTP_REFERER: Provides the address of the page whence the request originated.
- HTTP_USER_AGENT: Specifies the name of the client program used to make the request.

Script Output

After a script has obtained all of the information from the server and done any necessary processing, it must return its results to the server. In contrast to the multiple ways in which a CGI program can receive data, it can only return data in one way—by printing information to standard output. Similar to the HTTP response sent from server to client, the CGI script's output must consist of a set of headers, followed by a blank line, followed by any relevant message body.

Output Headers

When the server sends its response to the client, it creates a variety of HTTP response headers that provide information about the connection and the content delivered in the message body, as shown in Listing 4.2. For static documents, the server has all of the information it needs to generate this header information. However, as we discussed in Chapter 1, a script needs to provide a `Content-type` header line to inform the server of the Media Type of the script output. Listing 4.5 shows a script[9] which returns an image; before sending out the file, the script ensures that the `Content-type` header indicates that the Media Type of the data is `image/gif`. The two newline characters (represented by \n\n) that follow the `Content-type` separate the headers from the image data that follows.[10]

Listing 4.5 This script reads a picture from a file and returns it to the client; the `Content-type: image/gif` line tells the client how it should process the data.

```perl
#!/usr/local/bin/perl

require "cgi-lib.pl";

open(FILE, "pic.gif") || &CgiDie ("Couldn't open file pic.gif: $!");
print "Content-type: image/gif\n\n";
while (read(FILE, $buf, 16384)) {
   print $buf;
}
```

_____

[9] This script actually has a few new things in it. `FILE` is a filehandle; that is, an object which contains information about an opened file. `CgiDie` is a routine in **_cgi-lib.pl_** which produces a complete error message; it will generate a `text/html` `Content-type` header to ensure proper display. The `||` means "or," and here it is being used according to Perl idiom: if the expression before it is true, the second is not evaluated. The `$!` is a special variable which stores error messages—in this case, it would indicate why the file open failed. Finally, the `read` function is an effective way to read binary files.

[10] Technically, the HTTP draft specification indicates that header lines should be terminated with carriage return and a newline (\r\n), instead of just a newline. However, while every server seems to recognize \n as a valid termination character, at least one has difficulty when given \r\n. Therefore we violate the standard in favor of what works.

Upon receiving the script output, the server parses the `Content-type` header line and uses it to synthesize the appropriate HTTP response headers that are sent back to the client.[11] The server adds a status line, as well as the `Date`, `Server`, and `Content-length` headers to the information returned from the script. However, the script is not limited to providing just the `Content-type`. The server will also parse two other header lines if they are given as part of the script's headers, and it will use them to alter its response to the client; these are the `Status` and `Location` headers.

The `Status` line is used to specify the HTTP status code that is returned to the client. As shown in Listing 4.2, these codes take the form `nnn text` where `nnn` is a numerical status code and the `text` is a human-readable string that further explains the result. While the text associated with each number can vary from server to server, the numerical codes themselves follow a convention laid out in the HTTP specification. Of all of the codes listed in the table, however, only a handful are of real use to script writers.[12]

Table 4.1 HTTP Status Codes

Code	Name
200	OK
201	Created
202	Accepted
204	No Content
300	Multiple Choices
301	Moved Permanently

---

[11] The server parses the `Content-type` line returned from the CGI script in order to create its own version for inclusion in the HTTP response. Thus, while the header returned to the client should look similar to that generated by the script, they might not be identical.

[12] Scripts are not prevented from returning any code, defined or not (for example: `450 Confused`). However, if the client does not recognize the code, it will treat it as the x00 code for that category; e.g.; a 450 code would be interpreted as 400.

Table 4.1 HTTP Status Codes (continued)

Code	Name
302	Moved Temporarily
304	Not Modified
400	Bad Request
401	Unauthorized
403	Forbidden
404	Not Found
500	Internal Server Error
501	Not Implemented
502	Bad Gateway
503	Service Unavailable

The most common status code, 200, indicates that the request was accepted and fulfilled, and that the requested information follows in the message body. For a GET or POST operation, this might include the requested resource or the output from a script. For a HEAD operation, the headers are returned with no message body. As the server will generate the 200 code by default for any script which completes successfully, it is generally not necessary for scripts to use a Status header.

"No Content," indicated by status code 204, specifies that the request was valid, but there was no information to return. When the client receives this result, it should do nothing, as though the request had never occurred. Scripts which process clickable images will frequently return status 204 to indicate that the user clicked on an inactive area. Because users may be confused when their clicks do not generate any results, it is best to use this status code sparingly.

The standard description for code 302, "Moved Temporarily," is a bit of a misnomer. In practice, this code is generally used any time that a script redirects a request to a new location.[13] The location itself is specified in the aptly named header, Location, which the script must also supply when

---

[13] If a page has permanently moved to a new address, status code 301 should be used instead.

returning this status. Indeed, the `Location` header and 302 status are so intermingled that if a script specifies a `Location` header without a `Status` line, the server will generate a status 302 instead of the default 200.

Typically, when a client receives a redirection, it will automatically issue a new HTTP request for the URL specified in the `Location` header. From the user's point of view, it will appear as if he or she had jumped directly to the new location, instead of executing a script.[14]

Most of the other result codes apply to specific cases or error conditions and are generally not returned by properly executing scripts. In particular, most of the error codes in the 400 and 500 categories are returned automatically by the server. If the script encounters some internal error, it should output valid HTML text that indicates what went wrong and allow the user to take the appropriate action to fix it. The ***cgi-lib.pl*** library provides the `CgiDie` and `CgiError` subroutines to make this easy. When called from within a script, `CgiError` creates an HTML page from the string it receives as its parameter; this can be used to display an error message. `CgiDie` does the same, but also exits the script.

Besides the `Content-type`, `Status`, and `Location` headers which are parsed by the server, any other headers returned by the script will be passed along to the client with no modification. Of particular interest to script writers are `Expires`, which indicates a time after which the information should be considered "stale," and `Content-encoding`, which specifies any encryption or compression that has been performed on the data. Scripts could also supply any made-up headers, like `X-Foo`, and the client will ignore these if they are unrecognized.

A Picture Is Worth a Thousand Words

Often, a single script will return different status codes, depending on the input that was passed in. Clickable images are a particularly good

---

[14] Of course the new location itself could be a script. If this script issued a redirection back to the original script, it would cause an infinite loop; the HTTP draft specification indicates that most clients should have logic that prevents this problem.

example of this usage. As their name implies, these are pictures that the user can click; different locations on the picture correspond to different Web pages. The user can retrieve a page simply by clicking on the appropriate area in the picture.

Clickable images are commonly used in interactive Web games and in navigation bars, as in the example in Figure 4.1. This bizarre navigation bar contains three active regions and one area which does nothing at all. Clicking on the "Left" area produces some text, while "Home" and "Help" redirect the user to other pages. Clicking on the "Nothing" has no discernible effect, since the browser displays no new content. The HTML code used to generate the navigation bar page is given in Listing 4.6; the source code for the CGI script that processes its results is shown in Listing 4.7.

Listing 4.6 The HTML source for *navbar.html*, which contains a navigation bar. Notice that the form for the navigation bar contains no submit button; a click on the image itself submits the form.

```
<html>
<head>
<title>Navigation Bar</title>
</head>
<body>
<h1>Navigation Bar</h1>
<p>Please click on the bar below to go to the appropriate page.</p>
<form method=GET action="navbar.cgi">
<input type=image name="navbar" src="navbar.gif">
</form>
</body>
</html>
```

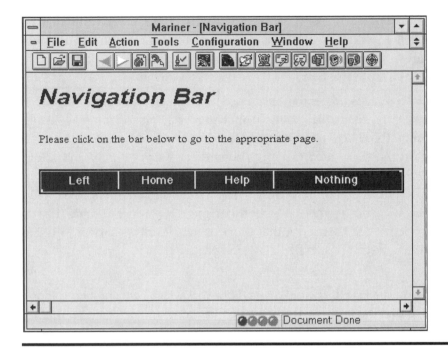

Figure 4.1 Navigation bars are often used as a convenient way to allow the user to jump from one part of a Web site to another.

Listing 4.7 This CGI script *navbar.cgi* outputs a variety of different headers to tell the server how to respond to clicks in the navigation bar.

```perl
#!/usr/local/bin/perl

require "cgi-lib.pl";

MAIN:
{
  &ReadParse;
  $x = $in{'navbar.x'};

  if ($x < 100) {
    print &PrintHeader;  # Status 200 will be generated automatically
    print &HtmlTop("Thanks for clicking!");
    print "<p>Congratulations, you've clicked on the far left of the ";
```

```
      print "navigation bar!</p>\n";
      print &HtmlBot;
   } elsif ($x < 200) {
      print "Location: http://www.mycompany.com/\n\n";
   } elsif ($x < 300) {
      print "Status: 302 Redirection\n"; # clearer description of 302 code
      print "Location: http://www.mycompany.com/help.html\n\n";
   } else { # $x >= 300
      print "Status: 204 Do Nothing\n\n"; # ignore user's click
   }
}
```

The script determines where a user clicked by examining $in{'navbar.x'}. Since it doesn't care about the vertical position of the click, it ignores $in{'navbar.y'}. Depending on where the click occurred, the script branches to different pieces of code.

If the user were to click in the "Left" region of the navigation bar (i.e., in a position within the first 100 pixels), then the script would output a typical HTML page. Note that, as with all of the previous scripts in this book, the Content-type header indicates the Media Type of the following text. The server automatically generates the other appropriate HTTP response headers and returns a status code 200, indicating success.

Clicks in the two middle regions cause the browser to be redirected to one of the following URLs:

```
http://www.mycompany.com/
```

or

```
http://www.mycompany.com/help.html
```

Note that two different methods are used to produce this result. If the click occurs between pixel positions 100 and 200, the script produces only a Location header; from this, the server knows that it should automatically generate a 302 status message. Clicks between positions 200 and 300 also specify a Location, but here the Status is explicitly given. In both cases, when the client receives the redirection status, it typically issues a new request for the resource specified in the Location header, taking the user to the correct page.

Finally, if the user clicks all of the way to the right, the script will return just a 204 status. This result tells the browser to do nothing, as if the user had not clicked anything at all.

Using Image Maps

The `<input type=image>` form element is only one way to create a clickable image. The simplest way, of course, is to create a hyperlink that highlights a picture instead of text:

```
<a href="http://www.mycompany.com/page2.html">
<img src="http://www.mycompany.com/arrow.gif"></a>
```

A click on the picture of the arrow would whisk the user to the page specified by `http://www.mycompany.com/page2.html`.

This approach does not, however, give us any information about where in the picture the user clicked. For that, we need to make a couple of modifications. First, we add the `ismap` attribute to the image element. This causes the position of the user's click—in the form x,y and expressed in pixels from the upper-left corner of the image—to be appended to the URL as a query string. Second, to process this information, a script must be specified as the destination URL. The hyperlink would therefore look like:

```
<a href="http://www.mycompany.com/click.cgi">
<img ismap src="http://www.mycompany.com/map.gif"></a>
```

A click in the upper-left hand corner of this image could generate a request for a URL similar to:

```
http://www.mycompany.com/click.cgi?10,20
```

The **click.cgi** script could then retrieve these coordinates from the `QUERY_STRING` environment variable and respond appropriately. This approach would be similar to having an `<input type=image>`

element in the form, except for the difference in the way the click position was reported.

A more common way of processing the results of such an image (often called an *ismap*, after the image attribute) is to use a pre-written software program called `imagemap`, which is typically provided with the server software. Imagemap programs basically take the place of your own CGI scripts that process the click location. Rather than producing any HTML themselves, they just return redirection messages—useful for navigation bars and the like. When specified as the destination of an ismap, the imagemap program uses a configuration file to associate regions of a picture with URLs; depending on the region of the image clicked, they redirect the browser to the appropriate page. Imagemap programs are not standardized but are generally available for most server platforms. You should consult your server's documentation and the Online Appendix (see Appendix D) for additional information.

Notice, however, that all of the approaches we've seen thus far—imagemap program, form input, and query string—are quite inefficient when called upon to simply provide redirection services. The browser first contacts the server with the click coordinates. The server, with the help of CGI programs, then determines the click position and returns an appropriate redirection message. Finally, the browser must retrieve the data at this new URL. Netscape 2.0 adds a feature to short-circuit this process by allowing the client itself to do the click-to-URL-mapping. Called *client-side image mapping*, the process has been proposed for inclusion in a future version of the HTML standard.

While client-side image maps cut the server out of the loop altogether and therefore have nothing to do with CGI, we feel that they are very valuable and deserve some discussion. There are two parts of a client-side image map: the map itself, given by the HTML element `<map>`, and the image which references it. Both are included in the HTML document, so the client does all of the image map processing. For example, the following map divides a 45 pixel wide by

20 pixel high image into three equal-sized horizontal segments, each of which is specified by a rectangle.

```
<map name="salutations">
<area shape=rect coords="0,0,  14,19" href="/hello.html">
<area shape=rect coords="15,0, 29,19" href="/hey.cgi">
<area coords="30,0, 44,19" href="http://www.yourserver.com/hi.html">
</map>
```

Note that the `shape=rect` attribute is the default and therefore can be omitted, as in the last area specified in this map.

The image that uses this map would be specified in a manner similar to an ismap. However, the enclosing hyperlink is no longer necessary and the `ismap` attribute is replaced by a `usemap` attribute which specifies the name of the map:

```
<img src="map.gif" usemap="#salutations">
```

A click at image position 20, 10 would fall within the rectangle bounded by the points (15, 0) and (29, 19), so it causes the page `/hey.cgi` to be retrieved. The syntax for the map file is flexible, allowing non-rectangular regions and other niceties. The Online Appendix has details on where you can find out more about client-side image maps.

Because many browsers do not yet support client-side image maps, you might choose to include both `ismap` and `usemap` within a single image. In this case, if the client supports client-side maps, it will use the `usemap` and the specified mapping information; otherwise, it will access the server image map.

Non-Parsed Headers

Occasionally, a script may want to communicate directly with the client, without having the server parse any of the header information.[15] In this case, the script could be specified as a *non-parsed header* script. These scripts are identified by the server just like other CGI scripts, with one exception: their names are prefixed with **npb-** as in:

```
http://www.mycompany.com/nph-addr.cgi
```

Unlike scripts in which the server interprets the headers, these scripts must generate a complete header appropriate to the `SERVER_PROTOCOL` that is passed in. Most scripts are accessed using the protocol `HTTP/1.0` and must therefore produce the status line (including the protocol identifier), `Server`, and `Content-type` as part of the header. For scripts which return data in the message body, a valid `Content-length` should also be given.

Non-parsed header scripts are slightly more efficient than scripts which have their headers parsed, but because overall performance is usually tied to the speed of the network rather than execution of the script itself, non-parsed headers are infrequently used in practice.

Review: Using HTTP and CGI

While most users will never need to know the inner workings of HTTP and CGI, a little knowledge can be quite helpful in the creation of scripts that do more than just output HTML text. The basic information presented in this chapter should be enough for most applications and should prove to be a good background when consulting other references. The following are some things to remember in using HTTP and CGI:

---

[15] This is the case, for example, when the script does not want to buffer its response and is particularly important when using features such as Netscape's server push.

- The HTTP protocol specifies a request sent from client to server, and a response sent back by the server to the client. Together, a single request and its response make up a transaction.

- An HTTP request consists of a request line and optional header information, followed by a blank line. Additional information can be specified within the URL by using extra path information or a query string. For requests made using the `POST` method, a message body may also contain additional user data.

- An HTTP response consists of a status line, header information, a blank line, and possibly a message body. The server constructs the HTTP headers either by itself or by parsing the information returned from a script.

- Scripts access information from an HTTP request by using the CGI protocol. User data is available on the command line for isindex requests, in the `QUERY_STRING` environment variable for extended URL requests, or through standard input for requests made with the `POST` method. Additional information about the server and connection are found in other environment variables.

- A CGI script must output one or more header lines, followed by a blank line, followed by any necessary body data. In the header lines, the script can specify information pertaining to the message body, like its `Content-type`, or it can provide information in a `Location` header to redirect the client to a new address. The script may also specify a `Status` that is returned to the client.

- The following table summarizes the HTTP request headers. Most of these are parsed and provided to scripts in environment variables that are part of the CGI standard. Additional headers from clients are placed in environment variables beginning with `HTTP_`.

Table 4.2 HTTP Request Headers

Header	Usage
Accept*	Indicates that the client is capable of handling output of a particular Media Type. Most clients will send multiple Accept lines for the various types of data they can process. Many clients send */* to indicate that they can handle any type.
Authorization	Provides information that is used to determine if a user has the necessary permission to access a secure area.
Content-encoding	Specifies that the information in the message body is encrypted, compressed, or encoded in some special way.
Content-type	Indicates the Media Type of the information in the message body.
Content-length	For requests with a message body, specifies the number of bytes in the message body.
Date	For requests with a message body, indicates the date and time that the request was created.
From	Gives the email address of the user using the client, if available.
If-modified-since	Tells the server that it need not comply with this request if the document hasn't changed since the time given. This is essentially a conditional request, which is especially useful for clients which cache pages. Such a client would use this field to say something similar to "Get this page only if it has changed since the last time I saw it, which was 14 June 1995 at 9:03 am."
MIME-version	Provides the version of the MIME specification used to generate the message body.
Pragma	Contains any additional information that the client wishes to specify to the browser.
Referer	Gives the URL of the page from which the request was made (often called the *requesting page*). Note the misspelling of this header.
User-agent	Indicates the name and version number of the client software making the request.

*The Accept header is not part of the HTTP/1.0 draft specification but is in common use.

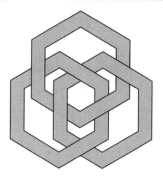

Solutions to Common Problems

While ***cgi-lib.pl*** makes it easy to create CGI scripts in Perl, the complexities of the interactions between the client, server, and script can lead to occasional problems here and there. This Appendix lists some of the most common problems encountered by beginners and experienced programmers in the course of creating Web applications. If the suggestions here don't help, you might also try contacting the system administrator at your site, reading the USENET newsgroup `comp.infosystems.www.authoring.cgi`, or consulting Appendix D for a pointer to additional information online.

General Troubleshooting

If your script isn't behaving as you think it should, try running it from the command line, making use of Perl's `-w` flag to display warnings for suspect code. You can simulate input from a form by setting the appropriate environment variables (see Chapter 4) and/or redirecting a file to standard input. If your script behaves properly when run manually, make sure that your server is correctly configured to run CGI scripts by trying to run other CGI scripts in the same directory. The other sections in this appendix and in Appendix B can help with this aspect.

If your script doesn't appear to be getting the input it expects from a form, check the HTML source of the form which calls it, making sure that all of the `name` and `value` attributes are correct. For comboforms, verify that you are correctly branching on `ReadParse` to determine whether to display the script or to process the form. Also, make sure that the form's `action` attribute gives the address of the correct script.

For scripts that generate HTML text, use your browser's View Source command (or the output generated when you run the script from the command line) to verify that proper HTML is being generated. You may want to try saving the output to a file and viewing that file in your browser, or use one of the widely available HTML-checking programs to look for any HTML problems.

Once you have a script that runs (albeit with bugs), you can use functions in ***cgi-lib.pl*** to produce debugging output that can help you track down remaining problems. The `CgiError` function can take a string as its parameter. This string will be output to the server for display in your Web browser. Because `CgiError` automatically produces the proper `Content-type` line, it can be called any time in your script, so long as you've included the ***cgi-lib.pl*** library:

```
require "cgi-lib.pl";
```

If you call `CgiError` more than once, your debugging output will be interspersed with additional `Content-type` lines. This may not be pretty, but it does not detract from the fact that using `CgiError` is an easy and convenient way to display information that could prove helpful in tracking down a problem.

If you're having a problem with forms, it may be useful to display the name/value pairs that are reported to your script by the client:

```
print &PrintVariables(%in);
```

This line generates and outputs a list of the user data that your script receives. PrintVariables does assume that the %in associative array has been filled in, so you'll want to call it after having called ReadParse. Also, unlike CgiError, PrintVariables doesn't generate header lines, so you will need to call print &PrintHeader; before displaying the output from PrintVariables.

Text of Script Rather Than Result of Script Execution Displayed

The source code of a script is displayed when the server, for some reason, doesn't realize that your script is indeed a script to be executed. Consult the sidebar entitled "Recognizing a Script When You See It" in Chapter 1 to learn how HTTP servers recognize scripts. Also see Appendix B for specific hints on configuring CGI scripts for your particular system.

Error 500—Internal Server Error (Misformed Header)

This error message from the server means that something has gone wrong with your script. Unfortunately, beyond the assurance that the server has tried to execute your script, there is not much more it will tell you. Often, you can get a little more information by looking in your server's error log; many servers record CGI scripts' STDERR output there.

The most common source of this error is that for some reason, the server did not receive the expected header information first. Most likely, this occurs because the Content-type header was not the first line output by the script. The headers, including Content-type, must precede any message body and must be set apart from the message by a blank line. The easiest way to ensure that the proper header is generated is to place the following line (or an equivalent one which prints out the appropriate Content-type if your script does not output HTML text) before any other code in your script that generates output:

```
print &PrintHeader;
```

PrintHeader returns the headers but does not actually print them, so you'll need to make sure that the call to PrintHeader is preceded by a print statement.

Even if the print &PrintHeader line does occur at the beginning of a program, however, it is still possible for things to go awry if your script calls any external programs (e.g., uses the system command). Because Perl output is usually buffered, the arguments to the print command may not actually be output until after the external program has run and presented its output. To solve this problem, Perl scripts can turn off output buffering using the statements:

```
select(STDOUT);
$|=1;
```

Disabling buffering is inefficient, so if large amounts of data will be output, it is preferable instead to simply flush the output buffer before calling any external programs:

```
require "flush.pl";
&flush(STDOUT);
```

A 500 error could also occur because of a bug in your program that results in a compilation error rather than actual execution of the script. In this case, the compilation error will usually be shown in the server's error log. Errors in scripts called via CGI are notoriously difficult to debug, so it is best to first make certain that your script operates perfectly from the command line.

There is one particular error which often crops up only when CGI programs are run by a server. This is the failure to find the *cgi-lib.pl* library. One solution to this problem is simple: in the require statement, give a full path specification for *cgi-lib.pl*.

Can't POST to Non-Script

The can't POST to non-script error is particularly infuriating because you *are* trying to POST data to a script. The problem is simply that the server doesn't realize that your script is indeed a script. Consult the sidebar entitled "Recognizing a Script When You See It" in Chapter 1, as well as Appendix B, for hints on how to solve this problem.

Access Denied
(Also Error 403—Forbidden)

There are two common types of problems which can lead to an access denied message. The first is simply that the file permissions are set improperly on your script. On a UNIX system, scripts must be set so that the HTTP server can read and execute them. This generally means giving them both world read and execute permission (for example, `chmod a+rx script.cgi`). Since the Web server must also be able to find the file, typically all directories above the script must also have world execute permission.

Another possibility is that your CGI script is trying to run in a region of the server in which scripts have been disabled. If you are the Webmaster, you can alter the configuration to allow scripts in your directory. See Appendix B for more information about configuration. Otherwise, the only solutions are to speak with the Webmaster or to run your own server.

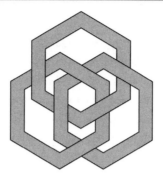

Configuration Tips

Virtually every HTTP server claims to support some variant of the Common Gateway Interface. However, since no two computers are set up in exactly the same way, it's likely that you will need to spend some time fiddling with configuration files to get everything working properly. The notes below, organized by platform, provide some basic information about setting up your server to run CGI scripts. Their focus is only on the details of enabling scripts in Perl; there is no attempt to discuss general server administration, security,[1] or compatibility. Moreover, because of the wide variety of software and hardware available, the methods listed here may not be appropriate for every version of server software or for your particular configuration. We therefore advise that you consult your server documentation and work closely with your Webmaster and System Administrator in order to ensure a trouble-free experience. The Online Appendix described in Appendix D provides additional information, as well as pointers to many of the software packages mentioned here.

---

[1] Enabling CGI scripts of any sort can introduce a significant security risk, particularly with scripts that make system calls.

Windows

The first order of business for most users will be to obtain a version of Perl that is native to your operating system. A number of public-domain Perl interpreters are available; in general, they are all named ***perl.exe*** and all work about the same way. However, the various Windows-based HTTP servers take different approaches to executing Perl CGI scripts.

The simplest servers to configure are those that automatically recognize the `.pl` extension in a URL as a Perl script. In order to execute a script, simply name your file with a `.pl` suffix instead of the `.cgi` we use in the book:

>   http://www.mycompany.com/myscript.pl

The server will search the directories specified in the `PATH` environment variable for an executable called ***perl.exe*** and will invoke it with the script name as its parameter. The EMWAC server uses this approach.

Some other servers require that ***perl.exe*** be explicitly specified as part of the URL. The script name is then appended as a query string:

>   http://www.mycompany.com/scripts/perl.exe?myscript.pl

Recall that for an isindex query, the query string is passed as a command-line parameter to the script given in the URL. The same thing occurs here, causing ***perl.exe*** to be executed with the file ***myscript.pl*** as its parameter. This operation is equivalent to what would happen if you were to enter `perl.exe myscript.pl` on the command line in order to have Perl run ***myscript.pl***. Perl scripts called in this way should use the `POST` method to send user data, since the query string is already used for the name of the script. On some servers, this approach creates enormous potential security hazards because it allows other users to download the source of your script and examine it for security holes. Far worse, it may enable clients to execute their own code on your machine via Perl's `-e` command line option.

Finally, there is the approach taken by servers like WebSite from O'Reilly and Associates and Win-httpd. These do not use CGI but instead write a file which gateway programs read for information. To use Perl scripts with these servers, you'll need to use a helper program like cgi2perl by Brian Jepson or Win-httpd CGI-DOS by John G. Cope These programs read these external files and create a wrapper around a Perl script, providing the script with information in a manner consistent with the CGI specification. They also pass the script's output back to the server. The Online Appendix (see Appendix D) describes where online you can find pointers to further information on CGI-DOS and cgi2perl.

As an aside, it's usually best to use standard 8.3 character filenames, even if your operating system supports longer names. Additionally, some servers will become confused with directory names that contain periods (i.e., `scripts.dir`), so these should also be avoided.

Macintosh

The most popular Macintosh HTTP servers are MacHTTP by Chuck Shotton, and its commercial version WebSTAR, by StarNine technologies. Writing Perl scripts for use with these servers is easy, especially when using the popular Perl interpreter, MacPerl. CGI scripts written in this environment can be compiled into small standalone programs, commonly known as *applets*, with the help of PCGI. PCGI, by Matthias Neerarcher, is an extension to MacPerl that provides Perl scripts with a wrapper (sometimes referred to as "glue code," or just "glue"). This wrapper translates AppleEvents sent by the HTTP server into the standard CGI environment variables and input. You can obtain PCGI as well as MacPerl itself via the Online Appendix described in Appendix D.

Once you've created your Perl script as a PCGI applet, you need to tell the server what to do with it. Because applets are simply applications, the suffix file type mapping section in the server's configuration file should contain the line:

```
APPL   .CGI   APPL *   text/html
```

This line indicates to the server that any file whose name ends in .cgi or which is an application (type APPL) should be executed and sent information via AppleEvents.

Macintosh servers do not typically place any restrictions on the location of a script in the filesystem, but because their view of the filesystem begins with the directory in which the server application resides, scripts must be placed in a directory beneath the server software itself.

UNIX

Partially because of UNIX's long history of supporting scripting languages (awk, sed, grep, and a wide variety of shells, to name just a few), and the fact that Web servers were originally developed on UNIX-based computers, CGI scripts are particularly simple to set up on UNIX systems.

Typically, UNIX servers come configured with a special directory called cgi-bin. Requests for files within this directory or its subdirectories serve as instructions to run a script. The NCSA and Apache servers set the precise location of this directory using the ScriptAlias directive in the configuration file srm.conf. The ScriptAlias directive establishes a mapping between an absolute filesystem directory on the machine, like /usr/local/etc/httpd/cgi-bin/, and an *alias* which is used in URLs to refer to that directory. As shown, the syntax is ScriptAlias, followed by the name of the alias and then the the directory path:

```
ScriptAlias /cgi-bin/ /usr/local/etc/httpd/cgi-bin/
```

Multiple ScriptAlias lines can be specified; each directory aliased in this manner will be treated as though it contains only scripts.

In order to enable scripts in directories other than those specified using ScriptAlias, you can turn on the ability to identify scripts by their extension. On the NCSA and Apache servers, this can be done by including the following line in srm.conf:

```
AddType application/x-httpd-cgi .cgi
```

Furthermore, you must enable scripts with the `Options` directive in ***access.conf***. You can, for example, set `Options All` or simply make sure that `ExecCGI` is one of the parameters specified on the `Options` line.

Of course in order to run Perl scripts, Perl must be available on your machine and in a location where the scripts can find it. The location of the ***perl*** program is given by specifying the full path to ***perl*** on the first line of the script itself, preceded by the `#!` symbols. In all of the scripts in this book, we've assumed that Perl could be found at `/usr/local/bin/perl`. A less common, though preferred, location is `/usr/bin/perl`. If it isn't in either place, you can use the ***which*** program to try to locate it by typing the following at the command line:

```
% which perl
```

If Perl is unavailable on your system, you will have to obtain and install it yourself.

The only other trick to enabling CGI scripts on UNIX systems is to ensure that the server can read and execute the script. Typically, this involves giving the file world read and execute permission, and ensuring that all directories above the script have world execute permission. Failure to set the appropriate permissions is one of the most common reasons for a 403 Forbidden error.

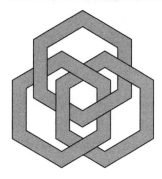

The *cgi-lib.pl* Library

The complete code of ***cgi-lib.pl***, version 1.14, is included in this Appendix. Because implementations of the `multipart/form-data` encoding were not standardized when this book went to press, the version of ***cgi-lib.pl*** given here will not process forms containing `<input>` elements of `type=file`. The most recent release of ***cgi-lib.pl***, which handles file-uploads, is available from the Online Appendix.

```perl
# Perl Routines to Manipulate CGI input
#
# Copyright (c) 1995 Steven E. Brenner
# Permission granted to use and modify this library so long as the
# copyright above is maintained, modifications are documented, and
# credit is given for any use of the library.
#
# Thanks are due to many people for reporting bugs and suggestions
# especially Meng Weng Wong, Maki Watanabe, Bo Frese Rasmussen,
# Andrew Dalke, Mark-Jason Dominus, Dave Dittrich, Jason Mathews
```

```
# For more information, see:
#      http://www.bio.cam.ac.uk/web/form.html
#      http://www.seas.upenn.edu/~mengwong/forms/

# Minimalist http form and script (http://www.bio.cam.ac.uk/web/minimal.cgi):
#
# require "cgi-lib.pl";
# if (&ReadParse(*input)) {
#    print &PrintHeader, &PrintVariables(%input);
# } else {
#    print &PrintHeader,'<form><input type="submit"> Data: <input name="myfield">';
#}


# ReadParse
# Reads in GET or POST data, converts it to unescaped text,
# creates key/value pairs in %in, using "\0" to separate multiple
# selections

# Returns TRUE if there was input, FALSE if there was no input
# UNDEF may be used in the future to indicate some failure.

# Now that cgi scripts can be put in the normal file space, it is useful
# to combine both the form and the script in one place.  If no parameters
# are given (i.e., ReadParse returns FALSE), then a form could be output.

# If a variable-glob parameter (e.g., *cgi_input) is passed to ReadParse,
# information is stored there, rather than in $in, @in, and %in.

sub ReadParse {
   local (*in) = @_ if @_;
   local ($i, $key, $val);

   # Read in text
   if (&MethGet) {
     $in = $ENV{'QUERY_STRING'};
```

```
  } elsif (&MethPost) {
    read(STDIN,$in,$ENV{'CONTENT_LENGTH'});
  }


  @in = split(/[&;]/,$in);
```

highest index of @in

```
  foreach $i (0 .. $#in) {
    # Convert plus's to spaces
    $in[$i] =~ s/\+/ /g;

    # Split into key and value.
    ($key, $val) = split(/=/,$in[$i],2); # splits on the first =.

    # Convert %XX from hex numbers to alphanumeric
    $key =~ s/%(..)/pack("c",hex($1))/ge;
    $val =~ s/%(..)/pack("c",hex($1))/ge;

    # Associate key and value
    $in{$key} .= "\0" if (defined($in{$key})); # \0 is the multiple separator
    $in{$key} .= $val;

  }


  return scalar(@in);
}



# PrintHeader
# Returns the magic line which tells WWW that we're an HTML document

sub PrintHeader {
  return "Content-type: text/html\n\n";
}
```

```perl
# HtmlTop
# Returns the <head> of a document and the beginning of the body
# with the title and a body <h1> header as specified by the parameter

sub HtmlTop
{
  local ($title) = @_;

  return <<END_OF_TEXT;
<html>
<head>
<title>$title</title>
</head>
<body>
<h1>$title</h1>
END_OF_TEXT
}


# Html Bot
# Returns the </body>, </html> codes for the bottom of every HTML page

sub HtmlBot
{
   return "</body>\n</html>\n";
 }



# MethGet
# Return true if this cgi call was using the GET request, false otherwise

sub MethGet {
  return ($ENV{'REQUEST_METHOD'} eq "GET");
}
```

```
# MethPost        At FSU, use POST
# Return true if this cgi call was using the POST request, false otherwise

sub MethPost {
  return ($ENV{'REQUEST_METHOD'} eq "POST");
}



# MyURL
# Returns a URL to the script

sub MyURL  {
  local ($port);
  $port = ":" . $ENV{'SERVER_PORT'} if  $ENV{'SERVER_PORT'} != 80;
  return  'http://' . $ENV{'SERVER_NAME'} .  $port . $ENV{'SCRIPT_NAME'};
}



# CgiError
# Prints out an error message which which containes appropriate headers,
# markup, etcetera.
# Parameters:
#  If no parameters, gives a generic error message
#  Otherwise, the first parameter will be the title and the rest will
#  be given as different paragraphs of the body

sub CgiError {
  local (@msg) = @_;
  local ($i,$name);

  if (!@msg) {
    $name = &MyURL;
    @msg = ("Error: script $name encountered fatal error");
  };
```

```
  print &PrintHeader;
  print "<html><head><title>$msg[0]</title></head>\n";
  print "<body><h1>$msg[0]</h1>\n";
  foreach $i (1 .. $#msg) {
    print "<p>$msg[$i]</p>\n";
  }
  print "</body></html>\n";
}



# CgiDie
# Identical to CgiError, but also quits with the passed error message.

sub CgiDie {
  local (@msg) = @_;
  &CgiError (@msg);
  die @msg;
}



# PrintVariables
# Nicely formats variables in an associative array passed as a parameter
# And returns the HTML string.
sub PrintVariables {
  local (%in) = @_;
  local ($old, $out, $output);
  $old = $*;   $* =1;
  $output .=  "\n<dl compact>\n";
  foreach $key (sort keys(%in)) {
    foreach (split("\0", $in{$key})) {
      ($out = $_) =~ s/\n/<br>\n/g;
      $output .=  "<dt><b>$key</b>\n <dd><i>$out</i><br>\n";
    }
  }
  $output .=  "</dl>\n";
```

```
  $* = $old;

  return $output;
}


# PrintVariablesShort
# Now obsolete; just calls PrintVariables

sub PrintVariablesShort {
  return &PrintVariables(@_);
}


1; #return true
```

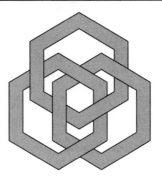

Online Resources

A number of online resources related to this book are available on the World Wide Web. You can access these resources at the following URL:

```
http://www.mispress.com/introcgi/
```

Among the resources you'll find are the latest version of the *cgi-lib.pl* library, source code listings of the example programs in the book, and pointers to many of the shareware and public-domain software packages we mention in the text.

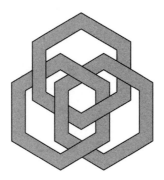

Index

A

arrays, 28
  associative, 35–37, 40, 51, 66
  Perl, 28–27
attributes,
  action, 58, 75
  ismap, 118–20
  method, 56
  multiple, 76
  name, 58–60
  type, 58, 60
  usemap, 120
  value, 58, 60

B

blocks, 23

C

CGI (see Common Gateway
  Interface)

CGI environment variables, 106–9
  AUTH_TYPE, 107
  CONTENT_LENGTH, 107
  CONTENT_TYPE, 107
  GATEWAY_INTERFACE, 107
  PATH_INFO, 107
  PATH_TRANSLATED, 107
  QUERY_STRING, 108, 118, 122
  REMOTE_ADR, 108
  REMOTE_HOST, 108
  REMOTE_IDENT, 108
  REMOTE_USER, 108–9
  REQUEST_METHOD, 109
  SCRIPT_NAME, 109
  SERVER_NAME, 109
  SERVER_PORT, 109
  SERVER_PROTOCOL, 109
  SERVER_SOFTWARE, 109

CGI-DOS, 133

cgi-lib.pl, 19, 23–24, 26–27, 30, 52, 53, 54, 57, 65, 66, 68, 81, 85, 89, 91, 92, 95, 106, 111 (fn 9), 114, 125, 128, 137–43

cgi2perl, 133

CgiError, 126–27

character classes, 46

checkboxes, 61–62, 93

clickable image maps, 87, 94, 114–15

client, 3, 4

client-server model, 3

client-side image mapping, 119

comboform, 69, 80–86, 91, 92, 102, 126

comments,
Perl, 21

Common Gateway Interface, 1, 8, 95, 131
definition of, 8 (fn9), 16
compared to Perl, 19, 52, 81–83

D

domain name,
fully qualified, 35, 40, 47
top-level, 35, 41, 47

E

elements, 28
<form>, 56–58, 92
<input>, 58, 60, 61, 77, 92; of type file, 88, 94; of type hidden, 90, 94

<option>, 77
<select>, 62, 75, 92
<textarea>, 77–78, 92, 93

encoding, 84–86

enctype, 57

errors, 126–29
access denied, 13, 129
can't POST to non-script, 129
Error 403, 129
Error 500, 127
Forbidden, 129
Internal Server Error, 127
Misformed Header, 127

extensions, 13

Extra Path, 100

F

flow control, 50

forms, 54, 60 (fn 5), 68, 92, 102

functions, 27
Perl, 20, 21

G

gateways, 8

Get, 56–57, 99, 105–6,113

global variables, 31

grep function, 83, 84

H

Head, 105

header, 5, 97, 110, 122–23
Accept, 97, 110
Content-type, 5, 23–24, 58, 99, 111, 112 (fn 11), 117, 127

Location, 114, 117
non-parsed, 121
output, 111–12, 122
PrintHeader, 128
Referer, 97, 110
Status, 114, 117
User-agent, 97, 110

here document, 34

hidden elements, 89–90, 92

HtmlBot, 39

HtmlTop, 32, 34

HTTP (see Hypertext Transport Protocol)

HTTP request, 96–98

HTTP response, 96, 98–99

Hypertext Transport Protocol, 4, 16, 95, 122
as a stateless protocol, 89
examples of, 3 (fn 2),
headers, 5
information flow of HTTP transaction, 7, 9, 10
message body, 5
server programs, 8
transactions, 58–59

I

image maps, 118–20

input, 9 (fn 10), 14

interactive pages, 53

isindex, 102, 132

J

join function, 85

K

key/value pair, 36, 60

M

MacHTTP, 133

Macintosh, 12, 133

MacPerl, 133

media types, 5 (fn 6)

method, 97

munging, 40 (fn 12)

N

name/value pair, 36, 60

newlines, 14

O

output, 9 (fn 10), 14

P

parameters, 29–30

password fields, 60 (fn 4), 93

pattern matching, 45

PCGI, 133

Perl operators,
=~ symbol, 42, 43
ampersand (&), 24
asterisk (*), 74 (fn 10)
at character (@), 28
backquote (`), 33
backslash (\ ), 45

carat (∧), 46–47

dash (-), 42

dollar sign ($), 25, 47

double quotes (" "), 32, 33, 37

hash sign (#), 21

match operator (m//), 45–49

percent sign (%), 35–36

period (.), 43, 85

question mark (?), 45

single quotes (' '), 33, 37

substitution operator (s///), 43, 85

substr operator, 48–49

translate command (tr///), 41–42, 49

underscore character (_), 30

Perl, 19

  arrays, 28–29, 35, 52

  as an interpreted language, 20

  compared to C, 20, 23, 41, 48, 81–83

  comments, 21

  functions, 20, 21, 52

  interpreter, 23

  libraries, 23, 24, 26

  metacharacters, 44

  quoting, 32, 33, 37, 52

  scripts, 21, 23

  strings, 52

  tags, 24

  variables, 20, 21, 25, 52

Post, 56–57, 97, 99, 104, 105–6, 113, 122, 129

PrintHeader, 24, 27, 32

PrintVariables, 66–67, 92, 127

procedure, 27

ProcessForm, 73–74

program block, 23

protocol, 3

Q

query string, 101

R

radio buttons, 61–62, 93

ReadParse function, 64–66, 67 (fn 9), 68, 74, 92, 126

regular expressions, 43

Reset button, 79, 94

S

scalar variables, 25, 28

  and Perl, 25

ScriptAlias, 134

scripts, 1, 8, 16, 63–68, 127

  as a gateway, 8

  calling of via CGI, 10

  filename extensions for, 13

  outputs of, 14, 16

  Perl, 21, 23

  server recognition of, 12–13

  with Web browsers and servers, 2

sed, 43

server, 3, 4, 8 (fn 8), 10

  and CGI script recognition, 13

  input of, 16

  recognition of scripts, 12–13

ShowForm, 73–74, 75

split function, 84–85

static page, 16

status codes, 112–14

strings, 28
   and backquotes (`), 33
   key, 36
   length of, 43
   Perl, 52
   within double quotes (" "), 32
   value, 36

Submit button, 54, 58, 63, 78, 94

subroutine, 27

substrings, 48

T

transaction, 96

typeglobs, 74 (fn 10)

U

UNIX, 12, 129, 134

V

variables,
   CGI Environment, 106–9
   global, 31
   interpolating, 32
   Perl, 20, 21
   query, 42
   scalar, 25, 28
   typeglobs, 74 (fn 10)

W

wantarray, 29

WebSite, 133

WebStar, 133

Win httpd, 133

Windows, 12, 132

World Wide Web,
   client-server model of, 3, 4
   diagrams of component
   interaction of, 6–7
   interactive pages, 53
   popularity of, 1